I0429306

Hail To The Second Best

Who Make The Best Prevail
(A Journey Unto Peace)

By Dr. Philip Stack

2012

Dedication

Hail to the Second Best is lovingly dedicated to the helpless children who, since the birth of the universe, God destined for them to be born, to enjoy the beauty and love of this world. Now many are made dead in the comfort of wombs by those enjoying being alive.....and heaven weeps.

The book is also dedicated to loving parents who, in their hearts, hear their new-born child speak: "Thanks for having me, Mother and Dad. You are the angels of my life; your soothing words and loving touch will be with me all days of my life. And what joy and happiness you give to me I'll share with others. I'll brighten the world with your love, and that's how God meant for my life to be."

This book is further dedicated to precious siblings.
The baby speaks to them: " Hello, Sister and Brother:
I have come from heaven so I can be with you.
Guess who I picked to love me? Your Mom, your Dad. and You.
I just opened up my eyes and guess who I did see?
YOU, I saw, standing there, looking right at me.
I have to do some crying, before I learn to talk,
and when you see me stretching, that's how I learn to walk.
See, my head wobbles all around, and my arms will go up, up and down.
I am brand new and I don't know what to do.
Will you show me how, so I can learn from you?
First I will have to eat; then I will roll over, and then I'll crawl and creep.
Soon we'll run together and play our favorite games,
and then we'll hug and care a lot 'cause we all have the same last names...
I love you."

A further Dedication is offered to your Family:
It's goodness time, our love is real;
It's sharing time, about how we feel.
When home is warm and life secure
The mind is innocent; the thought is pure.
Good tidings from our family and every kindness known...
We share with you God's greatest gift.
THAT PRECIOUS LOVE OF HOME.

Dr Phil's Greeting Cards
"We are Family"

Author

Dr. Philip Stack, a Psychologist, has devoted much of his life helping others with personal problems. He is married 54 years with 6 children and 21 grand children. "Raising 6 children for us was not that hard," he says.

He considers his wife to be fortunate to have him. Unlike most men, he is a romantic and considers every day a Valentine's Day. A son, already married for 30 years, approached him and confided: "Dad, the thing that you gave me that I appreciated most was, you taught me how to treat a woman."

Dr. Stack's book, HAIL TO THE SECOND BEST represents a search for peace through caring. He contends that many, many people are deprived of the simple act of being noticed. For example, he recalls noticing a female clerk at the airport. She was coughing. "You ought to be home in bed; you should take care of yourself," he suggested. Then he added: "I care about you."

"Why would you care about me?" the clerk inquired. "You don't even know me."
"Because you remind me of my daughter whom I love dearly," he replied.

What did Doc do? He allowed the clerk, a stranger, to feel the caring love of home. At first, when he merely saw her; she was second best. But noticing her as special, reaching out and giving concern, he lifted her up. She was no longer second best, but the very best.

Then she came over to Doc and corrected his ticket from 16A, coach, or second best to 6A, first class or very best.

Both strangers began in a second best position and each lifted the other up to a very best status: Hence, the title of this book: HAIL TO THE SECOND BEST WHO MAKE THE BEST PREVAIL; A JOURNEY UNTO PEACE.

Self-published & printed in USA by Tatay Jobo Elizes with Author's permission using Print-On-Demand System (POD) and Kindle Edition. Tatay Jobo Elizes is a Self-Publisher in USA. Published March 2012 under the ff. ISBN numbers: **ISBN-13: 978-**1470131371,   **ISBN-10:** 1470131374

Disclaimer: Views expressed by the author are his alone. Tatay Jobo Elizes does not knowingly publish false information or commit copyright infringement having been given explicit permission to publish this book. Tatay Jobo Elizes may not be held liable for the views of the author exercising his right to free expression.

Recommendation

Evaluation of "Hail to the Second Best"
manuscripts by Kathryn Knight

Fabulous. Intriguing. Well-written. WOW!

Content: This story was such a great fun to read, that I read beyond the allotted few pages and read the entire 30 pages that you submitted. The characters arc well defined and quite amusing. The opening scene grabs the reader.

Style: Nice! I don't think I marked anything that I thought should be deleted.. Your writing style is clean, crisp and well-timed. You have no superfluous "stuff." 1 love the smart humor.

Pace: Good Pace. The reader is brought along effortlessly through the story. Good dialog. Nice clean, short details. Good dialog pace.

Mechanics: No major concerns. A few glitches.

My, my, my....you are a storyteller extraordinaire

A few things I paused on:

Capitalizing the names of professions, such as "Mayor" and "Engineer" when you were simply referencing the role (not using it as part of someone's title, such as Mayor Van Culp. I would de-cap these, unless this was an intentional style. I know that Charles Dickens often capped professions (and lots of other words, which is confusing to the modern reader) so it is truly your prerogative. But I would tend to de-cap these.

But, overall. I found this writing very engaging. Your story-telling style is simply marvelous. I listened to the tape you gave me (THE HUGS) and was further impressed. Have you sent any of these to literary journals/publishers as short story submissions? 1 hope it's OK that I have kept the tape. I want to listen to it again.

This really is publishable stuff you've got here. I hope my "red pen" marks are helpful in refining this...in hopes that you will submit to some publishers!

Very sincerely.

Kathryn Knight, Review Editor
Tennessee Writers Alliance

Endorsement by Alan Couch

Hi Phil,
Here's my blurb:
Philip Stack's new novel "Hail to the Second Best" combines inventive storytelling with real truth telling. He makes you scratch your head while eliciting laughter and more impressively your deep thought.

> Alan Couch, Director, Spring Hill Library, 144 Kedron Parkway
> Spring Hill, TN 37174, Phone 931-486-2932 ext. 401

Endorsement by Bo Robertson

Remember the phrase, "question authority"? "Hail to the Second Best" by Dr Philip Stack is a workbook on questioning authority...but in this case, what is in question is the authority of or own fundamental beliefs about our relationships.

The book is filled with examples of folks trying to better understand and challenge their perceptions about love and how we as human beings relate to one another. Questions about how selfishness and love are interrelated help a community discover universal truths and become more self-actualized. Often, the novel begs the queston of who is considered "Best" in our society and who is considered "Second Best". What makes us prioritize our values the way we do? Is Selfishness a virtue?

Dr. Stack mixes some of his real life experiences into parables about love and life. There are pearls of wisdom on every page like, "living was not only a rush into life's adventures...it was experiencing life and death simultaneously." And, nobody has value in this world, except what he means to someone else's self-interest. There are a variety of life situations that get the ideas across pretty clearly; chances are you'll find your own frustrations echoed on the pages a few times. Many chapters are divided into specific topics, such as couples, money, addictions, and self judgments, with several chapters devoted to exploring perceptions of love regarding children.

Questioning your own perceptions about love is never an easy process, but it seems well worth the potential rewards..stress..free choices, peace, and affection for those closest to you. I enjoyed the book a great deal and suspect everyone can learn a thing or two from its pages...

> Bo Robertson, Assistant Vice-President, Financial Center Manager III,
> 5/3rd Bank, 3008 Belshire Village Dr, Spring Hill, TN 37174.

CONTENTS

Preface

I would describe my book as a novel with pursuit. It is certainly a story with an objective but it is not a love story. The theme is a search for peace. The question asked is, how can you have peace with so many losers? The losers I call Second Best....And what part does a loser play in evolving a peaceful society? And what part do the winners or the successful ones play?

The struggles and search for peace would appear very difficult because of the observed self-serving desires in human nature. People would rather stomp on each other to get ahead. Sad but true.

Nevertheless, an objective of the book, Hail to the Second Best, is to observe the impediments to peace and see how the hopeless, the forlorn, forgotten and hurting in society can be lifted and fitted in by having acceptance, meaning and value.

ORKWAY

"ALL YE WHO ENTER HERE ARE DOOMED FOREVER."

This was Orkway, a rocky repository for criminals and the coldest, most ominous, most unfriendly structure in Bullfinchtown.

A button is pressed. From behind an enclosed window Hal's head pops into view. Instantly, the steel door springs open with a loud "BUZZ." The weary group stumbles through the first gate. "CLANG," it locks behind them. "Another "BUZZ" opens a second gate. Past the huge Day Room, down a corridor flanked by prison cells they bring another resident.

"What number?"

"Sixteen." replied Hal, as he pursued the lawmen.

But why did he come to Orkway? Because he violated the good taste of his community by standing in the street naked. If only he were satisfied with that offense. But, no, being placed in jail he promptly tore out the plumbing....

At 32, he had gone completely haywire.

His wife left him. She left him. then whammo...bananas. Is it so difficult to believe that he became irrationally disturbed because a mere woman took a powder? Burt, Hal's number one assistant, was dumbfounded. "Me," he mumbled. "1 wish my goddam old lady would leave and take all the kids with her. I want to live in peace for a change." For Burt it was eating and hunting. Both had equal appeal, and he was not likely to exist without either. When he was saving up to make payments on a new 30-30 and had to cover an insufficient-fund check written by his daughter he was ready to ship his whole family to Siberia.

Now Len, assistant number two, just lived for his fifteen-year old daughter. His salary as a guard on Orkway was insufficient to take care of his domestic needs so he worked nights at a meat market. Occasionally, he brought snacks of tiger meat and blood sausage for the others to sample.

It was Hal, Burt and Len who represented the basic working force for the day shift. Three "guards" were needed to staff Orkway adequately. There could be more than three but not less: it was the rule.

Rules on Orkway were the province of bald Doc Proud, Psychologist and cigar-chewing-smoking addict. Since insanity was a common plea among the criminals on Orkway, Doc was required to make a Psychological assessment of their mental condition and submit a report to the judge.

ORKWAY, THE GENESIS

Orkway was named after Orkway Van Culp, Mayor during Prohibition. The original intent was to construct an art museum adorned with white English marble. It would have a lobby with paintings of the masters, Boticelli, Degas, Cezanne and Matisse and two ascending, white marble staircases leading to ten chambers on the second level. Each compartment would depict portraits and personal mementos of political figures who helped shape the town of Bullfinch. The intent, however, did not come to fruition. It was the second level, in particular, which was unacceptable to Mayor Orkway Van Culp. With some sinister plan in mind, the Mayor had a hand-carried distillery made. By placing the bait appropriately, suddenly important political figures who enjoyed imbibing were being charged with moon shining, an offense tantamount to murder in some religious circles. There were already twenty, from dog catcher, school master, to tax collector, who had sentences to serve....

But now, the town was facing a problem. A place of confinement was required for the rapidly growing, refined law breakers. The plan for the art museum was suddenly scrapped and replaced with a prison to contain the town's corrupting villains.

Some say Mayor Orkway Van Culp needed his name on something., then he systematically eliminated any political opposition to the idea. Others say he was perturbed because the others withheld election support. Yet others claimed he grew rich on a deal where all that museum money with its intended chandeliers, colored-glass figures of famous painters, paintings, and two marble staircases, was poured into a square chunk of rock, with nothing left over. Significant damage occurred in the Mayor-ship of Orkway Van Culp. There was no peace in the political arena, money was missing and the townsfolk were in disarray. Years later another Culp, Seth Culp entered the race. .

He was not him and he was not related to him, Seth insisted. He was Seth V. Culp, not "Van Culp." Cautiously, the voters believed it but they wanted more from a Mayor. "Peace," he said convincingly, "my platform is to bring Peace to Bullfinch Town." With a banner depicting a white dove in his hand and a peace platform on his lips, Seth V. Culp marched on to a squeaky victory.

How could he give impetus to that peace quest of Mayor Culp? Doc Proud wondered. He knew that an empty Orkway would be an ideally peaceful answer, but how could he, with a wife and six children, advocate that which would also eliminate his job? Living relatives of those early political figures wanted to see Orkway bulldozed to rubbles, not for peacefulness sake or even out of aesthetic necessity but because it carried a name they despised.

A 'LOVE' SURVEY

During contemplative moments Father Abe, a Catholic Priest, wondered, "Where is the love in Watergate?" The scene was replayed on the stage of his mind in many forms, the setting where firm loyalties existed once and were replaced by enormous contradictions; where there was binding friendship once but now, recrimination. Those who were useful and could he used had value or purpose. If not, the factions would split. "He is the naughty one, not me," each would contend, because to be naughty was to anticipate punishment.

Father Abe was convinced that somewhere, in the Watergate drama of life, love could be renewed. As a shot in the dark, he requested that a poll be taken. Mayor Seth Culp agreed to a survey tapping the diverse opinions on the meaning of love.

Letters were sent out to every tenth person in the town; the solitary question, "What is love?" Within one week 90.percent responded. Love was a pizza pie or holding a baby kitten. It was truth, sex, caring, sacrifice, a trip. God was love. Love was a "left-handed twiddle." It was a clean house. For 15% love was caring about someone or something. Ten per cent favored "God is love," 35% wrote "Love is sex," and 5 per cent cast their vote for hard work and responsibility.

Assessing the findings, Father asked earnestly, "What is the secret of restoring love to Watergate?

Harvey Calsbeke, a lawyer, saw the drama of Watergate as patently loveless as the time sentence which was, for him, the ultimate condition of lovelessness. For him it was a total loss. With the time sentence nobody wins and, as a final reckoning, the taxpayer pays for it all.

Harvey called love "a connivance, a crowbar at the service of the ego." Isidore Krasno, the youngest of the peace committee, an auctioneer, agreed with Harvey

Calsbeke about the "Crowbar Theory." He attested to its earliest use in courtship. "During lingering romantic moments, love thoughts were desperately spouted, hard and fast, like a woodpecker whacking away at some vulnerable tree, a salesman needing to make a quick sale.

Speaking personally, he said...."The love-spooning would die out after marriage. Now that you've won your prize, the flower shop would cease delivery.

At three in the morning his baby daughter would cry. He pretended that he didn't hear a thing. When Queenie nudged him, he'd pretend he didn't feel a thing. . His love-making created for him a child, a child whose greatest talent was making unpredictable noises, the ruination of all comfort zones and cozy habits commonly associated with a single life.

Suddenly, Isidore had a flash of insight "Let's stop the hurting in Bullfinchtown."

But Father Abe was in a gentler frame of mind. He wanted to believe in the expressions of love, in the nice things people did to help each other, preferring to accentuate the beautiful and good part of mankind.

"But the plan would eliminate hurting forever in Bullfinchtown," Harvey stated, with certainty.

"I could not believe there is that much hurting," Father continued to insist.

With a hardy resolve, Harvey stepped forward bullishly: "This is the plan...let us find the hurting people in the town and....."

"Care for them and love them." Father Abe suggested.

"Not quite, Father. We'll find the hurting people first. Then we'll assume that some selfish person is present, causing the problem. After we locate him, naturally we'll say, "Don't be selfish. He will heed the request, stop his selfishness and the hurting will cease."

The Mayor dubbed the idea "clever." Giving the sky above him a smile, he looked up and imagined a bright, white dove, suspended over Bullfinch Town Square, the only town in the world with such an honor.

Father Abe stood hunched over, not at all in harmony with the harsher proposals of friends, languishing in the sweetness of life. There was no trace of hurting in him. He positively felt that everyone was cast in the same unselfish mold.

DOC PROUD'S PRECAUTIONS

The time granted in the large Day Hall represented a milieu change which was mentally helpful to the caged inmates. Yet within that area there needed to be a regulation. Some could have 5 minutes to walk around or look out a different window; others could have one hour of card playing. One may be out alone; two may be out together, but not more than two. Some could be out twice a day, others only once. Of course, all wanted to be in the Day Hall for every possible moment. To permit everyone that token of momentary freedom simultaneously would create a serious hazard. Twenty against three would be horrible odds. What would the likelihood of peacefulness be in that place?

Doc would see who complains. Is he a constant complainer? Do the facts warrant the complaint? If not then is it necessary to suspect another motive? Then comes the judgment: how much freedom is appropriate to give that one, and what if he has already complained to the Governor.

What about the youthful resident who looks like the kid next door? The professional care will be attracted to this one instantly and receive a greater dose of understanding. He could have stolen 20 cars, burglarized three grocery stores and attempted murder. If he has a baby face and a nineteen-year old body, his mother will protect him to her dying breath. She will leave no stone unturned until he is declared crazy so her "baby" may not go to prison and may receive a social security check.

Then there was the red-headed one. The ventilating system carried voices which interfered with his reading and thinking. He had served three years of his sentence and was awaiting release. But he wants to kill the "Big Chief' who is responsible for sending him messages

Doc decided that the redhead did not wish to fill his lungs with the breath of freedom. "Free" had one meaning, to kill the "Big Chief' so he could be arrested and returned to prison. The red head would prefer to be insane than free. Woe to the man who feels like a nothing, a microbe. It is he who could burst into the limelight of sensational behavior. Call him a runt and he will stop your car, drag you from behind your wheel, and stomp on your face as if he were squashing an overripe tomato.

In contrast, see this one. He is free of the slightest twinge of aggressiveness. He hangs out with the tough guys who commit the crime. He's a patsy, a "Blame me" type. He'll even plead guilty to a crime he never committed. Doc asks him to strike his hand. His hand falls effortlessly, like a piece of flabby meat. Hearing a "Go to hell" he replies. "Maybe 1 should." He is willing to push a peanut with his nose. At twenty four he lives, but is dead. The chances of his causing a problem in the Day Hall. "Negligible," Doc Proud wrote in the man's chart.

This one writes a bum check for a dollar twenty to get some soap. Then he calls attention to himself by throwing a pencil at the clerk for refusing to cash the check. He has a fit if he doesn't get his way. The skinny kid in cell 7 is like that, a grown up baby. He wants his glasses right now. But no one has ordered glasses. Then he asks for cleaning fluid for his glasses...but he has no glasses. He decided he should have glasses or he will refuse to cooperate with staff....so he lays down with feet on the bed and head on the floor, and turns silent.

"Better cooperation required." Doc Proud wrote for this one.

Hal and Burt invited Doc to visit cell 12. Between cell 11 and cell 12, which were across from each other there was ample evidence of an excrement fight. A short, naked man was stooping down.

"Want to see it come out, Doc," he proclaimed with a sadistic glee.

"Why this?" Doc asked of his number one supervisor.

"The guys spread a rumor that he is returning to the pen today. He doesn't want to go."

"You're not going back...it is only a rumor...you stay," Doc Proud yelled. The man instantly, almost magically arose to his full height, donned his trousers and promised to clean up the mess. Surely, this one would not enjoy a Day Hall diversion until he kept his word.

A child molester has a legitimate fear of the penitentiary. To the other prisoners he is "Scum." Being mentally slow is a serious drawback and, if he is additionally a fat specimen, his inability to make fast moves makes it worse. .

There he was, with us, trembling, seeking reassurance over and over that he would not be sent to the Big House.

Unlike the excrement and child abuse situations, the young man in cell 8 demanded to go to the pen soon. When he deliberately stole his uncle's pickup and was picked up for speeding he volunteered to increase his trouble with the law.

"....and the truck is stolen," he reminded the officer who, until then, was only concerned with the speeding violation.

"And I have a loaded shotgun," he continued, compounding his difficulties. Why? Why was he forsaking freedom? Because "Free Life," as he called it had nothing to offer him. He was married and had a child from whom he was escaping.

"They will be better off without me," he decided.

Dr. Proud was certain that peacefulness required freedom and freedom was ushered in by harmony and getting along. In Orkway it was too dangerous to put a bunch of guys together. Most would not get along with even a little freedom. A peaceful social system was an impossibility here. Doc was convinced of it. But Orkway did serve the purpose of allowing others, who could handle freedom, to pursue it on the outside without interference from those who could not handle it. All those who came to this forlorn mass of granite were plucked from a society which was saying, "You may not fit here" while some others were saying, "We don't want you to fit here"

THE HURTING SURVEY

By noon, the following day, Isidore had distributed a supply of hurting posters. Each person receiving a poster was reminded to place it conspicuously on his front door. It was an ordinary red sign with two printed words, "I HURT."

During the second phase of the HURT HUNT Isidore and father Abe would be tracking down the posters.

An obese woman, in her fifties, pleasantly smiling, greeted Isidore at the door. Her mouth was crooked, the right side being drawn higher than her left. "Nobody in here hurts. We are all happy, very happy," she assured Isidore, casting a superficial, motherly, though crooked smile. Just then an ashen-skinned youngster crept up behind the obese woman, barely visible, peeking at the visitor.

"The sign on the door," she said weakly, "mother didn't know about it."

"Oh shosh. Lisa, nobody loves you more than I do." The mother brushed at the head of the youngster as if it were an irritating horsefly. "I'm going to buy you a new dress and I'm going to put a new door on your bedroom. Isn't that nice, Lisa?"

Lisa was quiet.

"I'm getting to like your brother Kirk a lot now."

"But you always said you liked me the best," responded the unseen girl who was clutching a cotton belt which girded the mother waist.

Isidore asked Lisa how she hurt, moving his head from side to side trying to get a good look at the girl.

"Oh, she doesn't hurt, do you, Lisa? We're good friends," insisted the mother, swaying her hips like a fat hula dancer, matching Isidore's head movements.

"I love my mother," whimpered the teenager in a whining, childish tone which clearly pleased the mother as she gloated, "see, I told you."

"But is there anybody who is selfish in this home?" Isidore asked, feeling if there was, then naturally someone would be hurting.

"Absolutely not," insisted the obese mother, as she closed the door slowly. "This is just a happy family, aren't we, Lisa?"

"Yes, momma." the girl replied, being forced back inescapably by her mother's huge rump. Before the door shut completely, the mother's chubby arm reached out, pulled down the piece of cardboard affixed there, and crumpled it.

Isidore held a straight, emotionless face as he left, intending to be completely objective about his Hurt-Removal Operation.

He sauntered across the street directing his steps toward another hurting sign which was posted on a door. There he came face to face with an attractive, blond woman who appeared to be in her forties.

"Does someone hurt in this family?" he asked.

"I do, I hurt," the woman replied without hesitation. Isidore was pleased at the invitation to "come in." In the living room he met the woman's husband, strong-looking, athletic, middle-sized. He was a real estate salesman who spent two nights a week at the YMCA keeping physically fit. One other night was for the Moose and two more nights out were for business meetings.

"Your wife is hurting," he told the man.

"Is she? I don't know why? The children are all grown up...all she has to do is take care of one boy." The boy had a palsy.

When Isidore posed his key question, "Any selfishness in this family?" the couple stared at each other.

A shuffling and tapping sound approached from the kitchen. A child appeared with crutches, dragging one leg. A huge head on the boy startled Isidore.

"Any selfishness in this family?" Isidore asked again. No response was forthcoming. Rising from his chair, he was prepared to leave but first he was forced to hear the virtues of the husband. He did not swear, gamble or chase after other women, "...and I earn a good living."

The recitation of the husband's magnanimous fetes followed Isidore clear to his car where Father Abe awaited him with curiosity.

Isidore showed no indication of being disheartened as both men drove off in search of more "I HURT" signs. When father asked if there was any opportunity to tell somebody not to be selfish, Isidore grunted, "Can't talk."

It was late in the afternoon. After canvassing the North Side, Father Abe expected Isidore to be feeling the strain. He expected some irritability, even a protest against committees of one...but he kept his cool.

Father Abe could not tell if Isidore was having a winning or losing streak with his hurt hunt as he swung his GTO to the South Side of town. He was looking hard, very hard for a red poster as Father sat comfortably beside him. If something was bothering Isidore, he contained it very well...until the next stop. It was so abrupt that father thought his head was about to be jerked off.

Father Abe turned to Isidore, wanting to be kind and supportive in spite of his own reservations concerning the horrors of selfish conduct.

"Forget it," Isidore replied brusquely, slamming the car door.

A young woman, about 25, seemed to be awaiting a caller. She opened her door prematurely before Isidore reached that very house. She had a cast on her left arm which extended from her fingers clear up to her elbow.

"I understand that somebody is hurt....." Before Isidore's words left his lips he was being grabbed by his sleeve. Out of a distinct sense of urgency he was being pulled to the woman's living room. From the basement emanated muffled sounds of children's' voices playing together as a short, bearded man entered from a narrow corridor.

"This is my husband. He is an Engineer."

The man was friendly enough, giving Isidore a favorable impression as well as a much needed optimistic feeling about the survey. For a moment, the sense of desperation of the woman left his mind.

"Why are you hurting?" he asked her.

Holding her distended abdomen with both hands she said, "We get into awful fights. 1 almost feel that I will harm somebody."

The woman held up her encased arm. "Do you see this? I drove it through the window."

With a sense of disillusionment, Isidore was curious to know if the husband loved his wife.

"I really do," The bearded man replied. Just two days ago we had a big argument. I said "1 love you." She said, "no you don't." I said, "I do...But we get along real good. We don't have any secrets from each other."

"One thing we don't do much is go out," complained the wife.

"She used to be a fantastic dancer," recalled the husband. Just then, four small children poured into the living room. At the precise moment when the noise was its loudest, Isidore sprung his prime question, "Anybody selfish in this house?"

All four kids were piling on the mother's lap.

"Anybody selfish in this house?" repeated Isidore.

"Definitely not," replied the bearded Engineer. "I love her.

Emma tightened her right hand into a hard fist, as if she was ready to break another window.

"I only know I love her and would do anything for her," the husband whined, as Isidore left the premises.

After six grueling hours on the road, Father Abe and Isidore were driving by another "I HURT' sign. Isidore slowed down.

"Should I or shouldn't I?"

"Tomorrow is another day, Isi."

Isidore held back, fascinated momentarily by the sign which was impaled on a picket fence. He vowed to make it a quickie.

Two people responded to his knock, A middle-aged husband and wife.

"Anybody hurting in this home?" he asked.

"We have a perfect relationship," the woman responded.

"We don't fight," the husband said categorically," and we never argue, not for thirty-three years."

Then a voice, emanating from the interior of the house was heard: "It's me; it's me. I'm hurting."

Isidore saw a very handsome man coming toward him, running the palm of his hand over his crew cut and chewing on a sandwich.

I don't know what to do with myself," he said. "Should 1 stay with my folks or find a job in another town?"

Isidore looked enviously at the Hollywood-Star Type, rugged, good-looking, neat.

"I was working with my dad in his body shop, but he kicked me out," continued the young man.

"It's just that you don't come to work on time. I can't run a business with you coming in any time you have an itching' to, Harry."

"He's a man. He should be on his own," declared the mother.

"Well, he's got a job with me anytime," said the father meekly.

"Every week I take a ride to the country to park. I say to myself, "should 1 stay, or should I go?' I resolve to make a change, but that only lasts a few days. I'm getting on my folks' nerves again. See, see...look at me. I'm raising my voice again...see? Son-of-a-bitch, my dad is ready to kick me out again...see?"

"Who is selfish in this family?" Isidore asked.

"Nobody," replied all three in unison.

Isidore thanked the family for its time and turned to leave.

Just then, the son requested a ride.

"Where to?" Isidore asked as both walked together crossing the street.

"The Funny Farm."

Without another word, the two men climbed into the GTO-Z. The car jerked forward with a loud screech. Driving faster than usual, Isidore headed toward the Southwest edge of town with Father Abe holding on to his hat.

It was the first hint of twilight. Isidore could see a wooden rooster perched atop a certain house on a hill as he slowed down. It had an arrow stuck through it and it turned in the direction of the blowing wind. Isidore placed that weather vane in that spot some years ago. He had also planted the red and purple petunias which lined the sidewalk and had painted that house white with a blue trim three times.

NEEDING LOVE

Baldy, the Hairball man in cell 5 needed love. He ate his own hair until he blocked his intensities and needed surgery. Consequently, with the help of a barber he was pronounced hair-free in all aspects of his being.

Herb the Verb also needed love. He could be heard rhyming in cell nine:

> "Shiv the niv in the sliv.
> Park your Cark in the dark.
> Get up here you fan of a lan
> Be mine and part my fart."

Herb needed his father's love. For being disobedient he was given three choices: he could stand on top of a coke bottle barefooted for an hour with no twitching with a shotgun to his head; he could run through the corn field for an hour chased by the family truck, or else he could wear a girl's dress for one week.

Herb the Verb is waiting for his father to change. Though a lot of people told him to strike back at his Daddy, he couldn't. It was unimaginable that he would destroy his only love resource. At times he would stop rhyming. Then he seemed to get more peaceful with himself. It was at that moment that he saw the light. It was all his fault. It was at that very instant he proclaimed, his cheeks moist with tears, "I love my Daddy."

In cell 13, which 50% refused because it was unlucky, was a real MD. He needed love so much that he tried to burst into the limelight. He broke into a motel room at 4 in the morning...just kicked in the door and stole two curtain rods because he wanted to prevent a robbery. The MD was looking for a good citizen's award but the judge thought a visit with the Psychiatrist was more appropriate.

The reborn Christian in cell 4 became a self-appointed Preacher. He was a former Alcoholic who needed love also. "Notice me," he sounded off every time he preached, and the preaching was incessant. The exact number was not determined but, conservatively, 20 "go to hell" notes were written on toilet paper, crumpled into little balls and tossed into the preacher's cell, rendering his religious fervor even more intense.

At Orkway the staff could not know for sure what dissension would occur between what combination of men if they were free of their cell confinement and permitted to interact socially. Those who escaped or attempted to escape would not be best associating with each other and those with a history of violence could spell trouble. Guys looking at 13 felonies or life sentences might risk almost anything.

Hal felt sorry for the Preacher Man. He thought he needed a dab of positive attention, some relief from the frequent spitball invitations to go to hell.

Doc perceived Hairball from a different viewpoint...a history free of violence. Consequently, the Preacher and Hairball were notified: "Day Hall, 15 minutes."

Five minutes after their release, Hairball, whose head had a shiny, cue-ball look stood erect. He placed his left fool against one of the 4 huge pillars which supported the 14 foot high ceiling.

The Preacher's eyes blinked twice just as a fist struck him at the bridge of the nose. Slivers of broken glass tinkled against the hard tile.. The body of the religious man slapped against the floor.

If the Preacher thought that a "God loves you" was sufficient to placate the bald man, it didn't work. "God loves you, Baldy," the Hairball heard, infuriating him. He grasped a handful of the Preacher's hair and attempted to lift him off the floor by it. He didn't succeed. In the process the Preacher's body became separated from his hair. For an instant it appeared that Hairball seeded bush-brown hair on his palm.

"Watch out," Burt yelled from inside the station as Hal tended to the preacher's lip and scalp wound.

It was too late. Hairball ate the Preacher's hair, every strand of it. Hal hoped he would not have another Hairball shutting down his intestines.

Doc Proud gave the externally hairless man freedom. Now it was being taken away, but something important was removed from the behavior of that person...trust. Something was also being added to the life of Hairball, cell 20, The Mummy's Tomb.

TILLIE PLOVER

Tillie Plover lived in the blue-trimmed white house on the hill. Throughout her life she was a staunch feminist and helped to defeat a number of prominent politicians who gave only the slightest hint on being wish-washy on the abortion issue. First she chose a career, then children. She never married because she would not be restricted by a traditional "piece of paper."

Tillie was proud of her independence and was guided totally by her own self-sufficiency.

Late in life, she gave birth to two sons, though it was rumored that she had three. She used her own parental style, preferring a one parent family and an unrelenting discipline. Going into puberty, her sons were totally out of control. As bad as they had become, Isidore Krasno, the popular kid in the neighborhood, turned out exceptionally good.

He met Tillie at the Super Market. He was a Boy Scout at the time. For some unexplained reason, independent Tillie allowed Isidore to carry her groceries. Later, it would please him if he could take care of her yard, then the house. Isidore actually looked forward to being told what to do by Tillie and showed not even a whisper of defiance. Tillie liked that in a man. Isidore knew what she needed and decided to play the part.

Soon Isidore felt as if he belonged to another family. He called Tillie Plover "Grandma Tillie" and would look in on her frequently. In subsequent years, with his own marriage, auction business and his participating in the Peace Program he was less available to Grandma Tillie.

THE REBELLION OF NATURE

Following the second day of fruitless selfishness-seeking, Isidore's constraint melted away. It happened in a glorious setting of a resplendent sunny day as he looked out of his bedroom window. An oriole fluttered among the branches of a white birch, the flowing water in the bathroom sang warmly and pleasantly in his ears. The day was beautiful aesthetically and sensuously perfect as delightful bacon odors perfumed the air. The moment was exquisite. All of God's creation seemed to be living in indescribable harmony.

Then nature rebelled. Without warning a commanding voice echoed across the land "So much and no more." Isidore felt weak, though his heart beat strenuously. No longer could he hear the water pouring in the bathroom and the sun turned gray. The birds adopted a new instinct, they demanded singing and, the beautiful white birch...it was marching in for breakfast. Then was manifest a most ghastly type of defiance which chilled the very bone marrow of the living...no clump of soil was willing to be nutritious for any tree that gave shade to any human being.

When the cold, gray sun demanded heat for itself and would no longer be a stove for the earthlings to warm their hand on, Isidore was frantic. He was seen building a huge chimney which was aimed at the silvery sphere and, from his own feeble breath, he fed it warmth.

Since Isidore could not lay his own eggs, he had none for breakfast, no meat, no bread. That glorious, nutritious milk of nature was gone. In a clear voice the fields once said, "Live, I am here for you." Now its words became sinister: "Without me you are finished."

He heard the sounds of neighbors in distress.

His eyes opened abruptly, his pillow drenched with perspiration. At last he knew. It was his own frightful moaning that he heard.

Shaken and groggy, Isidore struggled to his bedroom window, brushed aside the curtain and saw the tree, the white birch. It was in its place as always, reflecting the warm sun which caressed his forehead. Birds fluttered about in the tree playfully as the sound of rushing water was heard from the bathroom. The aroma of bacon frying in the kitchen relaxed Isidore. He was home and alive and nature was in its love-giving place.

Queenie Doll, Queenie Doll," he shouted out of sheer ecstasy and rushed to the kitchen into mothering arms which tenderly gave him refuge.

FREUD COMES TO ORKWAY

Sigmund Freud came to Orkway, beard and all. Doc Proud and the Freud simulator has some common interest, chewing cigars. Ziggy, as his Aunt Ariffa named him pleaded: "Don't do it. Doc, don't wock me in. I'w be good. I pwomise."

At least Ziggy was in one piece after holding off the police with a scythe near his mother's house.

"Doc, I'w eben bweg you."

Ziggy was kneeling before Doc, wanting to kiss his feet. His head went down; his beard brushed the floor. On his knees he was creeping toward a shoe occupied by Doc Proud's foot

"Excuse me," said Doc, removing a partially chewed cigar from his mouth, "I've got to spit." At that exact moment he felt a vice-like grip about both of his ankles. An attempt to take a step toward the toilet, not four feet away, was instantly aborted. Grasping onto the toilet seat was his only salvation as his body sagged out of control. He flinched at the awful taste of the cigar which he had reinserted, a portion of which he had inadvertently swallowed. He looked downward and spied where the other piece fell and, to remove the ghastly sight out of his mind, he groped for the toilet lid. There wasn't any.

"Damn it, don't they flush these toilets anymore?" Doc muttered as he pulled his shoes away from the lips that were trying to make love to them.

As Doc Proud left the cell for a moment, mostly to regain his composure and perhaps some dignity, Ziggy Plover, alias Freud held the cell gate ajar with his foot. He heard him say, "You pwomised, Doc; you pwomised on yew mothow's gwave."

A quick drink of water relieved Doc's distress and wrenching cough. He returned with a towel and tied the door to Freud's cell shut. The resident of that cell was pleased at the special treatment. He smiled almost affectionately, a soggy piece of cigar clamped tightly between his two front teeth.

"I wove you. Doc," he said fondly. To show that his gratitude had no bounds he serenaded his hero:

"Mewy had a widdle wam, wots of white snow, and wew Mewy went, the weaves would gwow."

'Want to heaw anothew one. Doc?"

"You wanted to kill someone with a knife?" Doc Proud interrupted, tugging on the cell gate to make sure it was firm.

"It was no knife, it was sheaws."

"Shears?"

"You got it wite. Doc."

Apparently Ziggy was cutting off the tails of small dogs as a hobby.

"Doggies wook bettew that way, Doc. Pwitty."

FEELING THE IMPACT OF THE RAMPANT "NO"

Isidore was obsessed with his squeamish dream. Having joined Harvey Calsbeke in town he immediately began complaining about that "Blasted survey."

"It's weird, Harv. I used to let things happen before, now everything's coming up selfish. See that corner?" Isidore pointed. "I was there yesterday in a real big rush...had to see a guy down the other block about a furniture consignment. I missed the deal by five minutes.... no more."

Isidore's arms dropped helplessly to his sides.

"It was hopeless...too many stupid corners... and Myra did have to buzz off with the car. What a lousy day to be visiting relatives. Nobody cares if it costs me five hundred clams, nobody."

Isidore asked Harvey to look at the mortar structures which snuggled together. "Life is freakish," he proclaimed, because yesterday he wanted to see a cornfield replacing one whole town block so he could conveniently cut across.

"The buildings were saying 'no,' Myra was saying 'no,' the guy who cut me short of time, he said 'no' and you, Harv...you bastard, you said 'no' too."

"Absurd," Harvey replied with surprise. The last time someone pointed an accusing finger at Harvey Calsbeke's nose was over 25 years ago, in the first grade...he wrote a four-letter word on his desk.

"Where were you at 4:45 yesterday?" Isidore yelled, grasping Harvey by the lapels with both hands and looked sternly at the bridge of his nose. "You weren't driving down that street and spotting me at 4:45 when I needed you and you weren't stopping and saying 'get in fast so's I can get you where you're going real quick.' No, you were hollering "no' just as loud as them others."

"I'm glad you don't make the laws, Isi," Harvey said nonchalantly as he brushed out some wrinkles in his clothing. "By your standards everyone would be in jail."

"It was your stupid brainstorm that got me playing hide-and-seek with signs so I figure I owe you a slice of my suffering."

If Harvey felt any abuse from Isidore the feeling which finally emerged was one of understanding. He was hoping that whenever he experienced "no's" they would always issue forth kindly, with plenty of spacing, not rampantly and in large doses. Above all, he thought, just as Isidore stepped into a waiting bus and both men parted on the friendliest of terms, how terrible it would be if someone followed him around all day and said "no" to everything he did.

Isidore was in an irascible, dominant mood when he arrived home. Being obedient to her better judgment, his wife entered the living room dutifully as her husband followed behind. It was in the chamber, just to the right of the fireplace, in a comfortable nook, that great domestic crises were resolved in the Krasno home.

"Sit down." Isidore ordered.

"Certainly, Discus." She obeyed, calling him endearingly by his nickname.

"You know, Myra," Isidore began, purposefully omitting the more sublime "Queenie" which he used copiously at moments when love and harmony ruled the relationship.

"You are just one in a million. Maybe you inherited some prehistoric genes...it's the only explanation. There I was, expecting you to get home early, just like you promised, but no. What happens? You pull in this morning."

"Well, 1 guess I'm selfish," Myra replied with total resignation as she calmly waited for the opposition to continue.

"I had a bad day yesterday because you had the car. I had to hoof it around town because you did not return as you had promised and what do you say? '1 guess I'm selfish?'

Pointing his finger at her nose, he continued: "Young lady, you are different. I can't tell you are selfish because you already told me. That is not fair. Why can't you be like other people, Myra? They don't want to hear that word. You frustrate me, Myra ...and you bring back this package, this thing..." Isidore points to something on the sofa. "And what's that?"

"A new outfit."

"A new outfit again? What in heaven's name do you have to say about yourself?"

"That I'm a little selfish?"-

"That's right Myra. You're damn right you are. You're a spendthrift, inconsiderate, a momma's girl, a dumb brunette...."

It was coming, Myra felt it: the inevitable, the predictable balm, the peace offering, the mending was about to occur about....now."

"But you are precious too."

"Ahhh," sighed Myra as she stretched out her arms to be greeted lovingly by the inevitable, "Kissie, big Queenie."

Myra wasn't surprised by the outcome. The ritual was all too familiar to her, but realizing that her husband made a special trip home to reconcile...."my, that was heavenly."

SECRET OF THE FOOT-LONG CIGAR

It was several days later. Doc Proud was making his routine rounds on Orkway. Hal handed him a foot-long cigar. "Number 3 wants you to have it"

"Once I won one just like it, at a carnival, for hitting 3 fuzzy wuzzy dolls with "a baseball," mused Doc, as he ran the large phallic symbol past his nose. "These smell better than they smoke."

"His wife brought it."

" Freud has a wife? Doc asked, surprised that he could take care of himself, not alone a wife.

"She's an Indian."

With the large cigar in hand, Doc Proud strolled leisurely toward cell 3. He passed by the suicide cell which, if occupied, was observed constantly by a guard through a mirror. It was indeed occupied by a twenty year old. His long, curly locks were hanging down idly from his cot. He was alive but he didn't want to be. Yesterday he spoke about his right to die so he could be a happy Prince and work with the Devil.

He wasn't scared of anything. When his Stepfather locked him in a refrigerator over at the junk yard, he wasn't scared either, 'cause someone shot some bullet holes through it and there was plenty of air."

Doc Proud's greatest challenge was keeping the suicidals alive.

There he was, Ziggy, the illiterate Freud. He was taking a nap following the noon meal. Doc saw a piece of cloth wrapped around his finger. Scanning the interior of the cell, he saw another, wrapped around a window bar, then another, around a leg of his bed.

Doc Proud continued to move down the corridor to cell 5. A short, young man, huge and flabby at the waist, wearing no shirt, which caused the fat to simply roll over his belt, was making snorting sounds.

His tray of food set on the bed. He rolled over just enough to shove the food into a cavernous mouth with his fingers, then he rolled over and chewed it. Back and forth he would go with one position for filling up and another for chewing. It was Len, the meat man, who characterized him as a "fat sow." When he came to Orkway the first time he complained that someone was stealing his pigs. This trip he complained that someone was putting pigs back.

"Get my cigaw?"

It was a familiar voice from cell 3. Doc took a few steps toward Charlesmagne Plover, alias Ziggy, alias Freud, and placed the cigar between the bars.

"Doc, I'w die if yew don't take it. My mamma bwought it. Doc. She's a squaw. Take it ow I'w kiw myself. Doc."

Doc Proud decided against returning the cigar. He asked the resident of Cell 3 about the cloth strip wrapped around his finger.

"Like my wing, Doc? I got won thew and I got one thew," he said, pointing to the window bar and leg of the bed. "Pwitty, ain't they?"

In the office the long cigar was barely being tolerated. First it was set near a pot of coffee; then it was seen near some Easy Rider Magazines. Just as Burt was about to discard it, he unraveled two pieces of scotch tape which were wrapped around it.

"Son-of-a-gun." Burt discovered a cigar sandwich.

Doc Proud, Burt and Hal left the office station in a hurry. The resident of cell 3 had shredded the towel which held the gate in place and strips of cloth were being wrapped around everything. But Doc was interested only in the wrapping on the window bar. There he discovered the midnight work of an escape artist. The bar was almost cut through.

Doc turned to the smug-looking, smiling fellow with the "Mewwy had a wittow wamb" bit and asked. "Where's the blade?"

"I ate it," he smirked.

Doc was impassioned to give orders in rapid fire: "Get rid of that cigar. No further visits. Find the blade and cleanup this mess." His final command, "Cell 20."

THE PEACE COMMITTEE RE-CONVENES

Isidore appeared in a frivolous mood at the 2 o'clock meeting of the Peace Committee. But his levity was concealing his disquietude, there being no reason whatsoever to suspect that his secondary attempt at hurt-sign seeking was any more successful than the first. He snapped open a large brown leather case and removed from it a pad no larger than the palm of his hand. Turning it over, he shook the empty case vigorously.

Isidore immediately apologized for his report. He had issued a hundred and twelve signs. Forty-two were fastened on doors, five posted on trees, two on fences, one was chewed up by a dog and he found fifteen on garbage heaps. In two days a total of 47 homes were visited. In all of them people were at home. Four told him to "get lost." Of the remaining forty-three thirteen residents invited him in, twenty-nine talked at the door and one conversed through a keyhole.

In 40 homes hurting was declared but nobody admitted selfishness. All claimed to be loving. Of those who claimed to be loving thirty gave living together as proof. Five said working hard made them loving and one asked "Why shouldn't I be?"

"If nobody's selfish and they're all loving, who am I to knock it," concluded Isidore, flinging his arms skyward.

Just a few days ago it seemed like a very promising enterprise to bring peace to Bullfinchtown. Now the Mayor's dream of a peace dove was shattered.

"There was selfishness in them homes like you wouldn't believe" asserted Isidore, but me? I wasn't going to tell them. I'd get killed. Like you can't just go up to someone and say, 'Don't be selfish'." They'll look at you straight in the eye and say, "Look buddy, I won't be and I never was." So where are you? Maybe selfishness and hurting go together, but the survey couldn't pin it down."

Isidore was surprised to hear Father Abe say, "It doesn't mean that no relationship existed, Isi. People could be selfish and not even realize it"

As a practitioner of Law Harvey Calsbeke understood how the opposite of love could be substituted for love and still be called love. Just as hate can mean love, the denial of selfishness could mean the presence of abundant selfishness.

"But why do people conceal their selfishness?" Isidore asked. "The trickery they devise to disguise it requires mountains of human energy."

He wished they could handle it like Queenie and come out with it; shout if off the rooftops: "Hey, down there, I'm 100% pure selfish"....Why not?"

"Because Queenie could afford to be selfish." said Father..

"Why?"

"Because you love her, Isi. Loving her, you accept her imperfections. You allow her to be selfish. You yell at her. you accuse her; you call her names; you swear and then....

"And then what?"

"And then.....

"I tell her she's nice."

"So why shouldn't Queenie call herself selfish. She is not a Watergate witness facing the prospect of a shattered life. If Queenie calls herself selfish she gets a predictable reward: "nice anyway."

"There is a trade however," Father pointed out, "she gives you the floor so you can holler to your hearts content; you give her a forgiveness that brings both of you back to your billing and cooing."

Harvey thought, if only he could have the knack of treating a loved one as "nice anyway," the same knack which came so spontaneously to Isidore, ..he...would ...even marry.

Father understood that considering someone as "nice anyway" involved a closeness to that person. The more valuable a relationship the greater the tolerance of imperfection.

But watching a stranger on TV who was involved in a scandal was totally different...there was nothing to lose. To him you could say cold-heartedly: "Let there be justice." You could afford to be careless, to speak with the lovelessness of the emotionally uninvolved GROUP MIND, insisting that "No man is above the law." The group mind responds in conformity with law which says, "Sad the protection is more important than truth," while the pleas of the dependently close is an opposite: "Sad that truth is more important than protection."

Isidore could see a basic discord, a clashing between the selfishness seeker and the distant, remote responsiveness of the callous group mind. Each demands his own way, but neither admitted being selfish.

"Cause it's wrong," bellowed father, fully informed by the thoughts swirling in his head.

"It kept me being nice all my life. From everything I saw and touched I expected niceness. With a feeling of regret and sadness father spoke from the depth of his being. "Isi, when I expected complete niceness, then I missed what was real. My selfishness was like a nose. I reached for it; I felt it. It was there. Then somebody ordered, "Don't have it, it's wrong/ The forbidding came again and again. It became stylish to wear a nose shield. I noticed everybody was wearing one. Then I put my hand under the shield...something was there. But I couldn't think it or say it because it was wrong to have a nose. I called it something else, maybe "love" or a "second head," but never what it really was."

"When the snazolla got stuffed up it felt terribly uncomfortable. Fortunately it never went 'Kaboom'."

Father reminded Isidore that the White House had its own Isidore Krasno on special duty. He also snooped around for selfishness, for hidden snazollas. "It was Laskeiwitz. He was most dreaded because if he found a snazolla he'd hold it up to public scrutiny. Exposing a drinking escapade, an illicit love affair or bribery had immense value. It could paralyze someone with fear. Holding up a snazolla you could even get life-long friends to say, 'I hardly knew him' and, if you had political ambitions, forget them. Being a powerful influence, everyone would soon begin hunting for hidden snazollas since they were as profitable as an oil windfall. Then, for everyone who raised his voice, that he had found one, two jumped up, protesting that the snazolla belonged to someone else."

"But why would anyone say that selfishness is wrong?" questioned Isidore.

"If it is wrong then there is a reason to blame others for having it," replied father.

"But who is the truthful person? Is it the one who blames or the one who is blamed?

"Whatever happens, it comes down to this: somebody wants his selfishness to be better than someone else's. Whatever Laskeiwitz does is naughty; what the Watergate Committee does is nice, but both do the same thing. Both are in the business of looking for hidden snazollas. With Laskeiwitz's snazollas the intention is to hurt and not care; with the Committee's snazollas there is no intention to hurt...but ultimately, both will hurt someone and both will not care. Of course Laskeiwitz was only in the filthy business of finding hidden snazollas but the Watergate Committee was on the ennobling mission of finding the truth."

"....And the latter is given the sanction and protection of law," replied Harvey Calsbeke.

After the Mayor plucked his tenth daisy clean from his one and only congratulatory plant sent by the staff of Orkway, Father Abe decided it was an appropriate time to leave.

All four were disillusioned. They were brought to the end of the road in record time. No doubt, the Mayor would continue to dream about his white dove. Harvey Calsbeke's humanitarianism, nurtured by his views against the arbitrariness of the time sentence evoked a spontaneous interest while Isidore Krasno's zeal for life allowed him an impulsive momentum which would not abate. Being stunned by the awareness of the omnipresence of selfishness, fascinated by the incongruity of labels, and irked by the invisible, abstract entity which reminded him daily, 'don't be selfish,' he was ripe for anything.

INCIDENT AT THE MUMMY'S TOMB

Burt and Hal escorted the wily Freud to the Mummy's Tomb.

Some who spent some time in Cell 20 experienced a sense of detachment, closed in, like becoming a wrapped-up mummy.

The door to the Tomb is ominous in its own substance, weighing 500 pounds. The steel on the door was a weave, no bars. You could cut for a year and not come up with a hole big enough to shove a hand through. In addition to an ordinary lock, in three spots on the frame of the door, a latch falls securely into place.

One last peek at Freud from between the weaves of steel created an instant panic among the 3 caretakers.

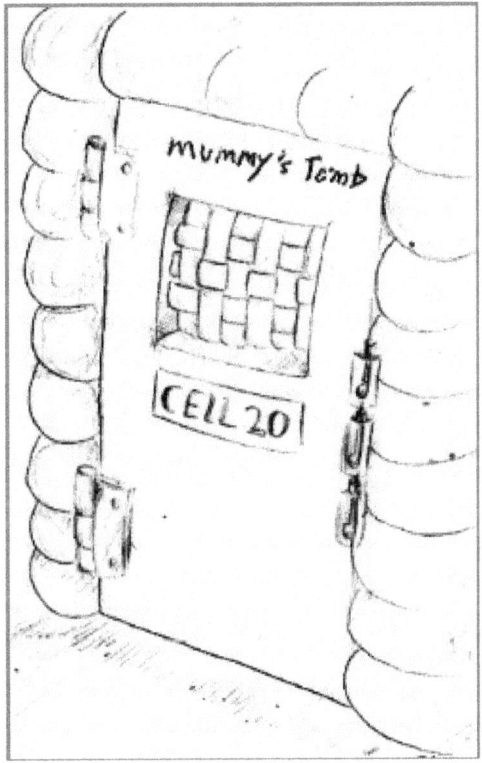

"Shoelace," Burt yelled. "He has shoelaces"

Hal thrust the key into the keyhole and cried out. "Maintenance, call maintenance," The key would not turn.

Burt ran frantically down the corridor to the office station to make the call.

Hal continued to try. The key wasn't working.

"Door's locked. Cell 20. We need help. Bring the torches. Guys hanging himself," Burt blurted into the phone.

The overlapping bands of steel afforded Doc Proud only a limited view into the Mummy's Tomb. His glasses were getting in the way as he changed slots rapidly, pressing glass against metal. Freud paid no attention to Doc's "I wuv you" tactic as he pushed the lace through the heavy metal screen which covered the full length of the north window at about the height of his neck and pulled the strands together evenly.

Doc fell backwards, feeling eyestrain, relinquishing his position against the door completely and landing unceremoniously in a sitting position.

"Thank God," he sighed. Then he began to laugh. "He can't tie a knot, Hal. Ziggy doesn't know how to tie a knot.."

Doc peeked inside the Tomb again...

"It's true," he said with glee." As hard as he tries he always comes out with two, separate, dangling strands of shoelace in his hands. No way could he fuse them into a hangman's noose. Even if he could, he couldn't fit his head into that little thing.

Being frustrated. Freud conceded defeat as he muttered weakly, almost humbly, and without a trace of the grin that told Doc that he was a victim of an unscrupulous illiterate, "Doc, I got cwastraphobia.'"

Two men with a tool chest came running down the corridor. In seconds a wide variety of tools were laid out on the floor. After inserting this tool in the keyhole, then that; after drilling and pounding for half an hour, the massive door stood, staunchly loyal to its purpose, firmly in place.

Suddenly the workmen discovered the simplicity of opening the massive door with the proper tool, a key. This time Hal had the right key for the job. His embarrassment would have been less profound if he had not thoroughly derided the maintenance crew for their ineffectiveness,

The thought of suicide could become so contagious and run rampant in the corridor of Maximum Security. But then, who would want to emulate the actions of Moronic Freud? Fortunately the kid in the suicide room didn't even know what was happening. Yet he was goaded by the Devil's voice to cease his earthly existence. Eventually medication helped him and the Devil's voice slowly faded out of existence. Only when he was fully crazed did he think of machine-gunning his mother but, when he was semi-improved, then he was contented that she would merely die of emphysema.

It was when he was much better then he loved her. He could not be normal, wanting to love her and machine-gun her at the same time. "What a complete twist of logic," Doc Proud thought. If only he could be crazy and only then love her or if only he could be normal and only then machine-gun her. He knew he would never see the day where the rules of craziness and the rules of normalcy would ever coexist in perfect peace and contentment.

Before the potential suicide left Orkway to face other charges in court he slipped one domino and one boiled egg into the Psychologist's hand. He wanted him to know that his dreams were happy now. In his last dream he dug up his mother's grave and found the body missing.

As for Freud, he did not make the Crazy Club, so read the report of the Judge. Doc Proud was glad to be rid of him. His clean 12 year record could have been besmirched, tarnished by a Moron. It made him shudder to think that he could have had a suicide if the Tomb occupant had an additional ten I.Q points to work with.

COMMANDING THE SHIP

Three days after the Peace Committee's meeting. Mayor Gulp called one of the four attendees.

"Command the ship," he asked.

Father Abe hesitated. "I am changing, but surely not competent. 1 couldn't be fair."

"...And we have a whole town to work with, Father."

Was it God speaking, or only the Mayor? Father gave himself a generous 5 seconds to decide the answer.

"I accept the challenge with conditions," he told Mayor Seth Culp. "My Bishop's approval and the reassurance that my selection is unanimous and not decided by an impersonal pluck of a daisy petal."

THE "WE CARE" NURSING HOME

The "We Care" Nursing Home was a one-floor structure near the edge of town. Hedges lined the walk to the front door and a small variety of weeping white birch was arranged in the form of a heart on the front. Dry leaves were gathered in unsightly clumps among the hedges and a row of poplars rose high above the flat roof on the North Side in an unsuccessful attempt to block the view of the Garden of Memories Cemetery just across Kidder Road.

Inside there was a beehive of activities.

"On the G, sixty four; on the B, two..." The sounds of Bingo could be heard inside as two men walked down one leg of a nursing home which was constructed like a spider. The center was a nursing station. If anything was happening down any of four corridors it could be seen from that central location.

The men residents listened to some hymn singing and then proceeded to the work activity area.

"Everybody works here...keeps their minds off their problems," said Mr. Peterson, the home's Administrator, as Isidore watched a strong, yet bony hand, pull a handle which crushed an aluminum can to a fraction of its size. In the next room were eight grannies working with the dexterity of a grand pianist. They encircled a bed spread which they held up with pride.

"How much," Isidore asked.

"At the craft shows they bring at least $50," replied Mr. Peterson as he backed out of the room.

"I mean, pay..."

'Oh, nothing...no pay is given. It gives the girls a chance to be civic-minded. It makes me proud to tell you that the girls worked hard to reach their recent goal. They finally purchased a new van and donated it to the home. Isn't that nice?"

Before leaving the "We Care Nursing Home," Isidore saw another group of residents stuffing foam inside some cute baby dolls and visited the Bingo parlor where the bulk of the residents were congregated. He learned that the monthly cost for a "civic-minded" oldster was $1800. Having looked the place over carefully. Isidore didn't see a single person in a wheel chair.

DR PROUD SPEAKS AT ST. MICHAEL'S

"Our subject for this evening is How To raise Perfect Children," announced Ariffa Plover, school board member and musical director of Ariffa's Ditties, an all-woman singing group.

There was premature clapping because everyone knew the speaker. When Dr. Proud was a student at St. Michael's High it was called the Peterson Township High School. The newly named St. Michael's Public School had a statue in front, the Patron Saint of Freedom. Hewn in the stone beneath the statue are the words, "Freedom of Conscience and Freedom to strive for Excellence."

"I am happy to present Danny Proud of whom we are all proud," continued Ariffa.

"I wish to thank the St. Michael's PTA for this opportunity and to thank Ariffa for her kind reference but, before I begin, I wish to clarify my topic for this evening. I will speak on how to raise good children, not perfect ones. I have my own kids, as you are aware and none of them are perfect. Please realize that I am not an expert in kid raising, though people often expect me to be. Being a Mental Health Professional is no guarantee that I will have well-adjusted children.

Doc glanced at the front row of seats. They were occupied by high school students. It appeared they were shooed to the front by the parents who undoubtedly expected them to be showered by wonderful words of wisdom.

"Let me tell you what I learned about child rearing," Doc stated, keeping one eye on the fidgeting first row. "For me, the first child was an experiment. I made mistakes with that one. I expected the child to need me abundantly, so I overindulged him. I spoiled that one; and what did I learn from that? I learned that children do not need parents as much as parents need children....at least those who are first born."

Curiously Doc saw one of the up-front students pull from his pocket an open bag of chips; another pulled out a can of pop. The male student with the can of pop had his eye on something. His gaze was moving up slowly, ever so slowly, then down. Then up again.

Doc Proud fought the distraction before him. He looked at his meager notes for the first time and said, "Moderation is an essential guide in discipline. I advise neither total obedience nor total defiance, but some of both. A child should never become so obedient in life that it becomes a weakness and every Tom, Dick and Harry finds him vulnerable and takes advantage of him. Neither should he become such a trouble-maker that his car is shot out from under him."

Doc. looked about the gathering of community folk and said with earnestness, "Most likely you won't get machine-gunned by your children if you follow them around to football games, recitals, spelling bees and stuff."

Doc saw some mouths agape...

"As long as they feel like a somebody, they won't kill you because they have too much at stake keeping you alive. And, if it means anything to you as parents, they won't go crazy out of wanting to kill you...so you'll keep them sane. And, if you are real fortunate they might even think of ways to keep you living longer. If you've got a kid who wants you to quit smoking because he's smart enough to know that nicotine constricts your blood vessels and makes your heart work harder, he probably wants you around to call him "Champ" or "Good Boy" a few times more or tell him to get his ass in by twelve."

The front row seemed to have settled down. Doc noticed. All, except one. He had opened the can of pop and was drinking from it but now, at that moment he moved the can upward, holding it carefully with two fingers. He quickly lowered the can of pop, placed his hand over the top, then he looked right, then left.

"Kids, you've got to let them be their worst where you can see it happening," said the Psychologist.

"I've got a theory about home. Home is where kids need to be allowed to be their worst, so that it can be corrected...that is making them safe for society. If the worse comes out in one place, then it doesn't have to come out in another. Society can influence kids by keeping them nice, in line, but there just isn't enough understanding out there to let them be mean, angry, or defiant....and that becomes the job of the home."

Doc was looking. He saw that familiar devilish look on the student's face but, surprisingly, the boy set the can under his chair...and that was that. Doc was certain that one of God's creatures, a fly, had been captured in that container.

He gave the can no further thought as he explained, "The kids have got to see the old lady and the old man fussing with each other, kidding around, kissing, hugging, whenever the urge grabs them. When they go to church they hold hands, like honeymooners and, if you're a kid in that family, you are damn lucky, because that's like a bell that chimes, telling you all is well in your home. When the home ground is secure, then it is easier for a kid to gather up all his resources, talents and abilities and go and tackle the battle of life. If parents show kindness, caring and good feelings toward each other, and the child senses this, then he will have the emotional foundation which will help make him a good person."

After responding to a host of questions, and the time was getting late, Doc was feeling tired. He approached the student with the can and asked, "What you going to do with the pop can?"

"Like you said. Doc, if you're going to do something naughty, you may as well do it at home...so I'm taking this pop home for my sister."

Doc Proud turned to find Ariffa's hand reaching for his. "We must have to repay you with a return visit, Danny Boy," she said charmingly. " Sometime my Ditties would like to sing for the poor boys at Orkway."

FATHER ABE PREPARES CONFRONTATION WTTH BISHOP

For two days Father Abe planned his strategy and mustered up courage for an inevitable confrontation with his Bishop. "What permission would I seek? Not that I was searching for an alternative to Watergate. No, not that. I need to offer a question of something, something magnificent."

Ah, yes, something spiritual, sublime," he spoke to himself as he spread grape jelly over a piece of toast.

Father, endeavoring to stack the cards in his favor, needed courage, strength and fortitude in abundance. He tried to recall someone in his life whom he admired.

Old Professor Hanel. The mere thought of his teacher excited him. He moved toward the fire place. Quickly he lifted a loose brick and removed a box and opened it. There it was. Hanel's picture. He brought it to the light, wiped it with his sleeve, and quietly recollected: If only he could be like him, only for the duration of his visit with Bishop Jewel.

Father gazed at Hanel's image, remembering his commanding, gentle voice: "A good Christian is for a precise moment only. He rarely lives as long as a Mayfly. If you say your are a good Christian or a good anything because someone assessed you thusly, then you were indeed that, but only for that moment. You mislead yourself if you believe that one compliment should have a lifetime guarantee."

Father recalled how convincingly Hanel spoke about life and love. He called the "I love you" as insufficient to justify love-giving.

"Any man needs to see what is coming back to him," he said. When he sends his love sincerely and hears from a beloved such words as, 'I feel inside that you love me,' then you are indeed hitting the target. Any man, by seeing what is coming back at him can authenticate his success in love and thereby know better the reaches of his love-giving power.

"God must love you because I can't go there to Him." Hanel scowled. "Wait!" he commanded us, and the scowl lifted. He was smiling, his arms extended fully to embrace someone. "Why go to God? Come to me," he said mightily. I have enough love for you all."

Hanel's world of beauty, of beckoning love would last forever in Father's mind. But his relentless, impactful courage enlivened his instinct to emulate the man. He could almost have the courage to love as he loved.

For two more days Father procrastinated, receiving continued encouragement from the Mayor to make a move.

Finally, Father Abe called Bishop Jewel.

THE ANGUISH OF TILLIE AND ISI

Tillie looked at Isidore with sad, pleading eyes. She beckoned him with *My Isi," then embraced him tearfully.

Tillie's left arm was weaker, Isidore noticed. It explained why she had difficulty steering her wheel chair.

'This is my home, Isi," she said firmly. "I won't leave."

"The nurse who visits you, what does she say?"

"I need more attention, but I know my home best. Someplace else I'd get lost. I'm going to stay right here."

Isidore was torn. He could not attend to Grandma Tillie and forsake all others who were equally dear to him.

"The nursing home on 12th and Kidder is very nice, they have Bingo, Arts and Crafts and Sewing...you like sewing."

"My eyes won't permit it; Besides, that's only for old people who are sedentary. I'm a whirlwind. It's in my nature."

Tillie's arm shook as she* tried to lift a handkerchief to her face. It fell away. Like a leaf, detaching from a worn tree, it landed on her left shoe. Isidore bent down and reached for the piece of cloth. Before he raised his head, he had tied the laces of both shoes.

Isidore was feeling guilty- He couldn't possibly hurt someone he loved, yet how could he see Grandma deteriorate in a place with no constant supervision.

"The nurse is with you but 2 hours a day. Grandma, but you need 24-hour care," he told her bluntly.

"How can you be so cruel, Isi?"

"It's for your own good."

"Get away from me," Tillie replied resolutely, waving her hand bye-bye at Isidore.

"You're no different than Ziggy and Zeph, them no good sons of mine."

Isidore was struck by lightning. His head drooped as his emotions flashed back and forth from anger to sadness...then pity.

Slowly he regained his composure and asked very softly, "You getting your meals brought in?"

"That part is O.K.," replied Tillie with equal softness.

"Want me to call the nurse or something?"

"That won't be necessary."

I'll come again soon Grandma. I love you."

Isidore looked at the HURT sign which he lifted from the inner lining of his coat.
"Who is hurting here? he asked himself, as he left the blue-trimmed white house.
"Grandma Tillie Plover is hurting here," he answered.

"Then who is selfish here?"

Isidore's mind went blank. He didn't want to know.

THE RUMINATIONS OF DOC PROUD

Doc Proud's narcissistic desire to be involved in the mainstream of life was being frustrated by a physical infirmity, a fiery-red throat He was disappointed in himself. Ordinarily he could detect those slight irregularities in his physical condition before they got out of hand.

He crawled into bed and turned the knob of the electric blanket up. Although his body relaxed completely, his mind was wandering.

That baby-faced kid flashed in his mind, the one who wrote to the Governor complaining about Orkway. In the investigations that followed, I told them repeatedly, "It was a manipulation, an insidious escape plan."

His baby face talked eloquently. Doc was no match being pitted against a broad Texas smile and a convincing commitment to obedience and law and order. He was rocking them lo sleep, divesting them of their natural alertness...and Doc knew it. Security was slackened.

Then the power surged through him and from him...until it was too late. Trampling under foot the obedience which he dangled before their eyes, he fled through a window.

Now it was "chicken time." Cars, on regular routes, were smacking into fence posts and landing in cornfields sideways. Battering a roadblock at a hundred, a shotgun blasted his radiator... yet he was not deterred. He worked hard getting behind that wheel...feigning epilepsy in Orkway, petitioning for better food. One eye was always open, looking for that pitiful look which told him he was convincing. Now he was making the big time, a real attention-getter, if he lived through it.

Finally, his tires shot out, he was bumped off the road.

He's back on Orkway. That ordinary, innocent look, the charm of the kid next door remains, waiting, patiently waiting for the next opportunity.

That evening Doc was at the game. Number 29 knew he was there; it was a contract written with the blood.

When that same 29, running like a gazelle, made a bee line for the ball carrier and dropped him on the three-yard line Doc could not have been anywhere else on earth and enjoyed a moment of excitement so thoroughly. On the sidelines, number 28, only a freshman, wanted to be a part of the action also. With that one. Doc felt empathy. He witnessed success as well as disappointment shared through the exuberance of youth.

Whatever risk Doc took with his health that night, he was satisfied. Deep in his gut he knew he had done himself a favor. He gave love to his children and received rejuvenation. He received the tonic which diverted his mind from his aches and pains.

The next day Doc felt better, but still recuperating. As the hour for the concert approached that evening, he was dressed. He was going because he wished to please someone he adored. He didn't care about his integrity, personhood, or even his opinion. At times he enjoyed being obedient to certain important people in his life. That being decided he would choose something for himself. He chose to be relaxed.

Following the concert Doc was happily rested. Surprisingly, everything he did for someone else, which he considered a sacrifice, turned out to be more beneficial for him. They benefited and he benefited. This he called "The Happiness Circle."

THE PEACE COMMITTEE CONVENES AGAIN

It was early evening. The moon was coming into full brilliance though it was shaped like a cradle. A light shone in the library of the Mayor's office. On a round, oak table, which matched the shape of the room, were a small bouquet of daisies inserted in a milk-white glass container and the evening edition of the Bullfinch Tribune. On this quiet, calm evening which might, with greatest appropriateness, be termed peaceful, four men came together. Father Abe, Harvey Calsbeke, Isidore Krasno and Seth Culp, Mayor of Knoe. The Peace Committee decided that the issues which concerned it should be brought to them through the newspaper boy.

Father Abe set the daisies aside out of the Mayor's reach, then opened up the folded paper.

"Funnies, I'll take the funnies. Father," Isidore requested.

"Anything else? How about ads, business ads?"

Father shook the paper and about a half dozen inserts fell out. Isidore scooped the business ads up and began reviewing them.

Father held up the front page. "Tragedies, problems, loneliness...you name it.....it's here."

Seth asked for a larger portion of the Bullfinch Tribune. "This will be for me and Harv...what's left?"

"Sports and Obituary," Father replied. "Anyone for sports?"

After some discussion, the Mayor and Harvey Calsbeke decided on checking the dictionary. Father finished the Dead People Section without any significant brainstorms, He nudged the comic strip over in Isidore's direction.

"What's your preference of search," he asked him.

"Honesty and fairness. What's Harvey and the Politician got?"

"Value and importance." -

"What does that mean?"

"Like making people feel they are worth something, Isi."

"...And you Padre, what's your line of investigation?"

"Guilt."

"Hey, that's pretty good," Isidore exclaimed, suddenly coming to life. "Should be right up your alley. You minister guys can throw that around like a manure spreader."

"Guilt," what a potent word," Father Abe thought "If you can't succumb by being hurt, maybe you can by being treated as if you have been hurting someone; If you can't succumb by being told to get out, then maybe you'll succumb if 1 tell you I will leave you and it's all your fault. I will even tell you you're not forgiven until I hear you succumb to the demands of my own selfishness."

Isidore was being both cruel and truthful. Guilt was a manipulation which Father used freely to coerce others. Now he was feeling a guilt pain of his own for having done it.

"God will love you if......" was his favorite.

Father was smarting, crouching in his chair. "Our quest is hopeless," Father said in a despairing voice.

Isidore noticed and instantly drew closer. "Buck up, friend, the town's census is merely 50,000...after all, you have me."

Meanwhile, Harvey and the Mayor were huddled together, flipping the pages of a dictionary searching for some of the nice words one can say to someone. They planned to offer a sign to the people, a GREAT BLUE SIGN and, with it, a message, a NICE message.

Hearing the plan, Father was a veritable turncoat when he said, "We live in a society where being nice to someone breeds distrust. You can't be nice just to me nice. The people won't believe it Harv."

"They'll believe it if they hear it right Father."

Father sensed that Harvey wanted his approval, not his opinion. On second thought, he agreed, that saying something nice to someone was not contrary to the interest of peace.

THE PLIGHT OF "THE GUARD"

'The bureaucratic red tape hasn't reached us yet. Doc."

"Damn it, it was a month since the escape, Hal. That baby-faced manipulator escaped, and what do we hear? Blame and inefficiency. That was our crack in the wall. Press one button and your accomplice is gone; press the other one and he's gone for sure. That was the sequence in the escape. Three, maybe four lousy seconds. No more."

Hal, Burt and Len were feeling disconsolate. None of them worked less than a sixty-hour week just for hand-to-mouth survival. They used to think that there was money in a name. "Technicians" was what they were called, but that had a tinny, cheap sound to it. Then came "The Guard." Now that was impressive. It had the sound of somebody watching, weapon in hand, saturated with manliness. They wrote the job description like a Dillinger movie and it paid off. They got a raise; the vast sum of 26 cents an hour. "That little high school crew did pretty good for cheap labor," thought Doc, with appreciation. "They wanted to be millionaires, and who wouldn't...and, by making comparisons with those they saw every day, at least they knew they weren't crazy...

Though their job was risky and unglamorous, it was real. None would be scheming to be picked on by the FBI, claiming harassment, and getting free disability pay for it."

FATHER ABE AND THE BISHOP

Leaving the Mayor's office late that evening, Father discovered that the valleys were made flat. Nature leaked a mist which leveled the terrain as it fitted exactly in lower places. By the time he reached the rectory and fumbled for his door key, the sultry, fogging air had reached his nostrils. He paused, remembering that solitary question which had sent him reeling out of orbit and thrust heavenward," The love in Watergate, where was it?"

Inside, Father Abe flicked a switch. The kitchen light shown, but differently. With a sense of life renewed and a purpose worthy of the gold of King Midas, he looked around. He was gazing beyond familiar wall plaster, excitedly telescoping the infinite universe. The horizons had horizons beyond them. Valleys were mystifying, strange, exotic worlds. Even the simple comfort of that small room was magnified in new discovery. He wondered if that was the feeling, the magnificent feeling which told him that God was pleased.

The light of father's bedroom flicked on as effortlessly as if he had never touched the mechanism. He looked! "Gods," He exclaimed with great restraint turning the light off instantly and staggering backwards into the kitchen. What he saw turned him pale. It was the Bishop, in his bed.

After a prayer to Hanel and a prayer to St. Michael, the Patron Saint of all seeking Freedom of Conscience, Father sat for an eternity anticipating the inevitable morning awakening. Without removing his clothes he lay down on a collapsible cot.

He began counting the thumping pulsations in his ears.

He saw a panorama of a Roman Arena. Male thumbs, female thumbs, large thumbs, petite thumbs, soiled thumbs. All were pointing downward. I'm not perfect," Father shouted to the crowd.

"Don't be selfish," they retorted.

"1 need protection." the priest screamed as the jaws of the lions came near. "Give us truth." the crowd demanded instead.

"Take me as I am," he begged them.

"Proof, give us proof," they responded relentlessly.

Father opened his eyes. The charging lions disappeared. It was morning. From the living room window he could see the sun beginning to parch away layers of fog as the nearby Veteran's Hospital marched out of the mist.

The Bishop, gaily twirling a loose end of a rope that girded his waist, made his entrance. After apologizing for the inconvenience, he explained that the caretaker let him in.

Father nervously prepared eggs, toast and coffee, while his guest did some stretching and bending exercises. After some mouth rinsing and toilet flushing both men sat down at the kitchen table.

"Hope you like the eggs. Your Excellency."

"I've always wondered about a Peaceful Society, Abe. What have you discovered? Is it truly possible for man to experience such perfection?"

Rubbing the ache off at the bottom of his spine with one hand and caressing the prickly stubble on this chin with the other, Father, pushing his shoulders back as if he were his own Chiropractor, said quietly. "The key to peacefulness in our society is still unknown to me."

Bishop Jewel's lips puckered. At his age he needed to see matters evolve overnight. That's why his very person was a surprise package, so he could ask that very question and receive a spectacular earth-shattering pronouncement.

Father was not disillusioned. However restless his night's sleep had been, it was a final sleep...and a beginning sleep; a sleep of death but also of birth; a sleep of dissolution and a sleep of resolution; a sleep of separation and a sleep of virgin embraces. There was no room for futility. Father was prepared to be arrogant for the sake of preserving his main ambition with the one person who could allow it.

"I found myself at a crossroads with my aspirations but now, more than ever, I am inclined to seek out in man some hidden answer to a peaceful society," Father said with compassion. He felt a momentary blessing as he looked at a glow of delight in the Bishop's tiny, piercing eyes.

"How will you proceed, Abe?"

"There is much to apply, but much more to know."

Father saw the unflinching "go on" look peeling away his resistance.

"It will require exceptional broadmindedness, Your Excellency."

"Me, I'm broadminded," the Bishop shot back, his appetite whetted. But Father looked at him. concerned that he did not have the necessary temperament to handle the information.

"Get on with it." the Bishop blurted.

"It may involve a complete reversal of principles we hold dear. It may involve a rejection of the importance of conduct."

My words had reddened the Bishop's face. A larger crimson blotch formed on the side of his neck.

"Good and bad. forgiveness, judgment may be true impediments to the realization of a peaceful society."

Father gritted his teeth following an awful scraping sound against the vinyl floor as Bishop Jewel rose abruptly to his full height.

"You subscribe to destruction, not a perfect peace. Ravenous termites is what you offer.. .scandalous."

The outburst produced a dizziness which forced the Bishop to drop into his chair. Pulling a string of brown beads from a fold in his loose-fitting garment, he began fiddling with them nervously.

"I am a horrible disappointment to you," Father said, speaking softly, compassionately, "but to someone must fall the inglorious task of finding the essential ingredients which together help constitute a peaceful society, even if that magnificent condition might exist but for an instant."

Father Abe wanted the Bishop to know how extremely difficult it was for him to depart from principles which he had staunchly embraced throughout his life. Now they had become weights on his feet, preventing his turning and looking in new directions.

"I could no longer cling to the old for the sake of the old. To be emancipated sufficiently from the repetitious past and to feel free to say I have endured confusion is difficult, but I welcome that stressful state, that place where every boy passes through to become a man and every girl passes through to her womanhood." The Bishop was unresponsive.

"It is one matter to sit in the luxury of truth and expect that truth will deal with the problems before us... it is quite another to continue to search for an even greater truth."

The Bishop pulled himself up from the table where he was praying as he continued to finger his beads. Placing both arms behind his back, and in that posture, turned and proceeded to study the goldfish design on the wallpaper.

Father Abe could not see his Bishop's countenance to study its meaning. "We have diverted ourselves to God, but God can take care of Himself. We cannot. We treat God as if He should be fed with our love until he is a fat Queen Bee. But we are the hungry ones. Let us provide love where it is needed. God is all love; He doesn't need ours.. We spend too much time making deals with God."

Father paused, clearing his throat, then continued....

"If the gates of heaven should suddenly appear on the horizon, half of humanity would trample to death the other half in their frenzied dash to get inside first. Those inside would lock the gates behind them. Soon half of those would be evicted by their own and, in a very short little while, half of the remaining, the self-chosen handful would claim sole ownership and those gates would remain forever shut."

The leader's face had a puzzled look, but not menacing at all. Silently Father prayed that God could be pleased with both, that both could be assured entry into His Kingdom.

"I need heaven and you need heaven," Father told his Bishop. "That is sufficient. Because man needs heaven, let him believe he has heaven."

Bishop Jewel's flushed appearance had subsided considerably. He nodded his head and, with only mild reluctance, admitted that Father's position was firm and sincere.

Both men were communicating privately. That was mutually comforting. They weren't speaking from a pulpit where surely many might suffer contamination and confusion. That sense of privacy prompted Bishop Jewel to dare to imagine how wonderful it would be, averting the next war where millions would suffer. That he could accept in the name of some unspecified peacefulness. He could even accept it if the method appeared a bit less traditional.

"What you think is important, Abe," was the most pleasant comment of personal value which Bishop Jewel could share. His parting words . "Be prudent, my son; be prudent in all things "

DOC PREPARES FOR THE TOMB

As Doc Proud's eyes scanned the oblong chalk board affixed to the wall in the office, he noticed it was being used for merriment of a sort as the trio sat snickering.

"Some entertaining human in our midst had decided to fun me," he said, referring to drawings of two unmatched socks.

"Just once, it happened," Doc protested lightly. Then he held his breath for a moment and listened. Some kind of bird was chirping. Doc never heard such a pretty sound before, not on Orkway. While he looked to the ceiling and all about expecting to see a canary, Burt, with a broad, diabolical smile, revealed an electronic bird which had been tweeting out of sight.

Some joking was fun. but for the boys to refer to Stubborn Stu as deceased was a deed most dastardly. It caused Doc to grab a Styrofoam and pour a second cup of coffee when one was his entire quota for the day. A reference to a dead body in a cell was not Doc's cup of tea.

Doc examined the check marks beneath each name. Eight out of 11 were completed.

Within a week these would be heading back to jails all over the state.

Christmas was fast approaching. Though Orkway had never been without somebody on Christmas Day, it had been consistently a lean period.

Hal had a premonition. "This year will be a good year, we'll be wiped out... empty."

Doc knew the wallets of his colleagues would likely register "empty" during the holidays. These three would surely be poorer this Christmas.

Hal began to think that the crime route was a sure-fire way out of his financial abyss. He had it worked out, first to commit the crime, get in the cell by Christmas time and get some of that turkey they always served with gravy and cranberry sauce. He wanted some of that good caring that he's been dishing out and felt he wouldn't mind gaining some weight either. He wanted to be fat and lazy for a change and not skinny and over-labored.

"You'll have to know how to act crazy," Doc reminded him. "Otherwise you could just land in some pitiful jail in some impoverished town and have a cup of dietary mushroom soup with crushed pickles." ,

Doc Proud checked the list of names again, there was no problem. Stubborn Stu had come out of it. remarkably on his own. but he plopped over a couple of times when someone told him to do something. He could tolerate being asked, but the telling dropped him like a hard blow on the head

Doc checked his valuables with Hal: watch, glasses, comb, which he placed in an envelope. He didn't expect any calls, nor did he need to make any. He checked a black book....nothing further was scheduled. Every thing was in readiness. He slipped into some loose-fitting bleached blues and a loose, oversized shirt. Finally Doc slid his feet into a pair of white, woolen socks and fitted them into moccasin-like. two-bit, flimsy footwear.

Unceremoniously, he was escorted to The Mummy's Tomb.

ADVENTURES OF ISIDORE AND MYRA

Future technology was the current theme at the Bullfinch Armory Exhibit. A large crowd was on hand to examine creations of the future.

Myra Krasno was there holding hands with her favorite man and excitedly pointing at practically everything in sight.

A miniature house came to her attention. It was a most peculiar part of the presentation because beams of light kept shooting down and the house was surrounded by intermittent bolts of lightning. Myra paged through a booklet. She glanced up at Isidore..."Lasers," she said excitedly, "the light is a laser."

"It's for the future, to keep robbers from breaking in. Fences are going to become obsolete."

"Come over here, Banana Blossom, look at this TV."

"My god," Myra exclaimed. "It's 3-D television."

"It looks so real. Feels like you're there. Gosh, this is exciting. Can we get one?" "Sure Honey Bee, we'll put our name on the list, right after we get back from the Mars junket"

Genetics was a subject of interest to the twosome. They looked at special displays under glass. Myra pressed a button. A voice began to speak about chromosomes, DNA, genes.."Genetic Programming" caught her ear. In the future it would be possible to program a child by gene alterations, blue eyes, red hair, tall, athletic, pug nose...

Myra turned to Isidore, and playfully grasped him by the neck with both arms.

"You are the greatest genetic programmer precious, nobody can pick a baby with the right parts like you can."

"Thanks, Honey Bunny. I just love the way you talk.

"Let's go over there. Look...what's that..." exclaimed Myra, pulling Isidore by the sleeve and dodging the milling crowd. It was the biggest something in the whole Armory, a long transparent submarine with living quarters and a garden with ripened vegetables...but no soil.

"A self-contained survival capsule is what it is. I read about it in the paper."

"But what's it for?"

"Survival."

"What's so special about that?":

"You can live in there forever."

"Dearest Darling, you're kidding."

"Not a bit Cutie Doll. You just keep recycling yourself over and over."

"Let's get one of those too. Dearest.."

"You want it, you got it, but first I'd like us" to go to Bullfinch Square ."

Isidore lifted a piece of newspaper from his pocket.

"Like to have some elegant, rose-petal china? Value, 500 clams."

"Yes...yes...yes."

After a bit Isidore and Myra Krasno entered Honest Dan's Car Place. They approached a desk occupied by a stately, well-postured secretary. Isidore cleared his throat twice before he received appropriate recognition.

"This is my wife," he said, "and I would like to have the rose-petal china set for ten."

"I'm sorry sir. those go with the purchase of a new car."

Isidore unraveled the newspaper and pointed to an ad, an Honest Dan ad.

The secretary pressed a white button.

"If a Pit Bull comes at us, we run," Isidore whispered to his spouse.

Myra brought her coat sleeve to her face, stifling her laughter.'

Isidore saw a door swing open just behind the secretary's chair; then it swung back. It flipped out a thin, lean man with a toothpick behind one ear and a pencil behind the other.

The secretary stood up.

"This gentleman wishes to buy a late model car, Dan."

Before Isidore could speak his hand was grasped and pumped.

"I'm Honest Dan...and what's yours?"

"Isi."

"Sissy?"

"No, Isi."

"What kind of work you do, Isi?"

"Auctioneer."

"Oh, I got a cousin doin' that in Kokomo, Jack Jeeps. Heard of him?"

"Like to pick up the rose-petal china, please," requested Isidore, coming to the point.

"And what kind of car did you wish to buy, Isi? The China goes with our latest models only. It's a rebate, our way of showing appreciation for your comin' in."

"Don't want the car, Dan. We're here to pick up the china. Right sweetheart?..no car."

"Right, Peaches Dumpling."

Honest Dan was stunned by the request of his two visitors. He turned to his secretary.

"Did you hear what I just heard?"

"This is not the Salvation Army," said Dan, emphatically. "In this place you don't get somethin' for nothin'. Let me tell you, Isi. you don't get nothing' free."

Isidore unfolded the newspaper again and held it up at Honest Dan's eye level.

"See it?"

"See what?"

Isidore pointed at one word in the Honest Dan's Car Place ad, FREE.

Do you see it now?" it says FREE CHINA."

"...with the purchase of a late model car. Read the whole thing Isi, the whole thing."

"But, Dan," Isidore replied, "If you must buy a car, then the china is not free. Why do you say it's free when it isn't free?"

Honest Dan had enough.

"Come back when you want to buy a car," he said, rushing through the swinging door.

Isidore glanced at the newspaper again, then asked the secretary to borrow a pen. He drew a circle around the Save-A-Million Clothing Sale and the "We Care" Nursing Home.

After apologizing to Myra for disappointing her, Isidore passed the pen back to the secretary.

"Keep it, he said, "It's FREE"

DOC PROUD LOCKED INSIDE THE TOMB

Doc Proud wanted the gusto, the bone feeling of the Tomb. He wanted to scan the environment from another's frightful eye and see in his own eye the same dread. He wanted to add meaning with depth to enrich his own feeble expressions of understanding.

The gaping jaws of the Mummy's Tomb widened on their hinges, waiting.

His head bowed, Hal and Burl escorted Doc swiftly down the corridor to Cell 20.

He would be segregated, a victim of his own desires.

Doc's first impulse was to push against the massive iron wall that slammed shut behind him.

In an instant his life experience shifted from the best of creature comforts to isolation, with one cot and one blanket.

Instinctively he began to examine his residence. To the West was a window. The mesh that covered it gave a minimal view of the sun, making a checkerboard design on the opposite wall. The Tomb was the shape of a square. Nine of his feet, one in front of the other, gave him the dimension. For some occult reason he multiplied 9 times 9 then promptly forgot why he did it.

Doc's eyes wandered. They scanned the monstrous steel gate. There was nowhere else to go, except up. To be a fly, would be great, he thought, moving about freely in that additional upper space. .

How to deal with hopelessness and the prospect of no escape was his objective.

"The window...God bless the window," he muttered. The sun's ray, even though split into fragments, contained a detectable warmth. Though winter was approaching, the meaning of the sunlight was magnified. It was life and its sustenance that Doc was reaching for in those dull rays and the hope that they would not leave.

He stood in the fast-receding sunset and carefully looked at the familiar laundry below. He watched for something shaking or moving...something with motion, even a scrap of paper blown by a breeze.

Then a laundry van came into view. Doc watched scrupulously as it turned around and backed slowly to a ramp. He saw the driver who began unloading some sacks of soiled linen...then he was gone. He looked over the buildings and saw farmland in the distance. It was long shorn of its produce and was lying dormant, waiting for another Spring to bring it back to life. The charm in nature's spirit was gone and with it the last flicker of daylight.

Doc again paced off the distance from wall to wall, then he did it backward. Either way it still amounted to nine lengths of his foot

He knelt on his mattress, sensing its softness as his hand moved caressingly over his heart He felt the thumping and the empty shirt pocket simultaneously. There was no cigar. He wished for the soil, humming sound of his acutron to entertain him as he held the cold nakedness of his wrist, compelled only to be warmed by the vision of the brilliant-red sunset which had totally receded.

The Winter of that day had come for Doc Proud. All that transpired elsewhere in the world was for another's gratification and pleasure, not his. Without light the feeling of neglect was at its worse.

Being chilled he tried several unheeded "fire-in-the-hole" yells. Then he sat down quietly, wrapping the blanket around him. He sat like an Indian defeated in battle, pining for Freud's foot long, if only for one sniff of it to feed the senses.

At home. Chick, son number two. would crumple his cigars. He wanted his dad to have more will power. If he could see his father now, a probing Surgeon, his fingers probing for a weak spot in the cot's plastic casing, discovering a rip and digging into the soft foam, to chew.

Spitting was a mistake. There was no water. ..no toilet either.

Doc had enough foresight to avoid a private humiliation. He willed constipation. Besides listening to the occasional faint sounds of shoes clicking against the hard floor and the muffled sound of a distant television, he listened for growling sounds within his body. Detecting none, he relaxed.

Doc had another dread...chow time. What went in would inevitably come out. He decided to eat very little. Later, his hunger could be accommodated by a tasteless piece of foam.

Doc Proud went down, the side of his head first, against the cot, testing for comfort. The rest of his body followed, curling up beneath the blanket

The night surrounded him. Up and down, he bobbed on a rudderless magic carpet that thrust him up. Halting, it jettisoned him into the recesses of a giant dome. It was the Grand Chamber of Vivian, the seat of judgment of societies. There the wisdom of many earth centuries and knowledge of myriads of civilizations was contained within a small green box which hummed with one solid pitch. High above the floor and along the sides were hewn entrances which matched exactly the proportions of the creatures who would enter that imposing beehive.

A dwarfish figure approached an entrance, hesitated momentarily, then passed in, with barely an inch to spare. Behind he left cotton balls floating in an intensely blue sky.

Through at least a hundred openings were dancing, bubbling colors which identified the exotic life-giving atmospheres of unknown worlds.

Some creature appeared. The figure, draped completely in a white sheet, gave greeting to the earthling. An antenna mounted just above his head twirled round and round. Then it slowed and wiggled, as if it were searching, smelling like a hound after the scent of a rabbit which scampered into one of a billion holes.

The creature was checking the biting, burning deserts, the polluted recesses of crowded tenements, ships and parked cars. He searched among pals and neighbors, gray ladies and in gay places.

For eons the creature had registered peaceful societies. The status of earth was now being registered in a large book with golden leaves. It read: "No peacefulness exists on earth."

Then came the thoughts, the criminal, decadent thoughts that creep into an unsuspecting mind, thoughts of violence, sex, conniption, of witches and embarrassing itches, of killing and being killed; the thoughts of unbridled, inner explosions. The creature called these virtues.

The earthling protested with thoughts of kindness and sweet things, of gentleness and cool springs. Defending even the freedom of the eagle he would then recline in a warm, browned meadow and rest.

The earth figure was treated disrespectfully. He was pushed, mocked, abused and diagnosed a killer. A bunch of keys dangled just out of his reach, to torture him.

His mind swirled in confusion as he sought to experience a personal attachment from which he could derive a sense of belonging. He saw shrines with loving inscriptions, love spices, love potions, Cupid, the child of love and African Love Flowers and, finally, food. Doc was hungry.

He woke to a whistling sound, raised himself up and came to the door.

His foot felt something on the floor, his meal.... one granola bar. Apparently they wouldn't give food that couldn't fit in a tiny, square hole. Besides, no one on the night shift would risk a confrontation with "The Killer."

No great stones were being turned for Doc while he slept. Now that he was awake he wanted to call all of them "bastards." They were beginning to look like useless college graduates with majors in nose-picking.

Doc wished for a periscope, anything to help him peer down the corridor. However, the flicker of the TV became his sole entertainment He tied his blanket against the door, forming a swing. In that makeshift hammock he sat. suspended a foot off the floor, his cheek against the cold steel, chewing his honey-dipped granola and being entertained by repetitious flickering. He was a damn petunia in the shade, reaching out toward noise and motion. The TV was being Doc's missing sun. But any knowledgeable student who could pump gas would know that a sun substitute without a toilet represented an environmental deficiency.

His knees began to ache and his butt was squeezed into an amorphous lump of putty.

It was time to urinate, but where? In spite of everything Doc was trying to consider good taste. He examined the corners of his cell thinking that modesty would require the use of a corner. They were all alike. If you spilled water in any one of them it would somehow flow right to the middle of the floor. If he urinated on his cot, the same result would occur. Of course if he could get the flow through the screen, he could use the window and not care if it dripped out and froze into icicles completely out of his sight. Maybe he could spare a moccasin, that dime piece of white covering which was made for shuffling, not stepping.

Doc Proud was through being coy. There was no worse cell, no Cell 21 to which he could be transferred for further security as his bladder was about to split in three. At that moment, increasing his power to act, he chose to be delighted that his parents allowed him to be defiant, at least in emergencies. If they made him obedient to the core then, maybe, he'd have trouble pissing out the door.

Then he urinated, out the door.

Doc ran his hand across the wall. He walked to the cold window and blew his breath on the glassy canvas. He tried to make an artistic stroke on the fogged-up glass. His finger was too short. He scraped a few loose flakes of paint from the wall, which were barely visible and played with them in the palm of his hand. Just then, the flickering ceased. The word "louder" reverberated down the corridor.

Doc instantly flung himself against the steel gate as if his skull would crack and squinted. He heard whistling. Unlike Burt's electronic canary, the whistling had no twitter.

Doc knew, only one person on Orkway needed noise to fall asleep. The Bellringer, Hacke Cramm, was back. He was being lullabied to sleep by, the guards. The only offense he ever committed was disturbing the peace with a bell. His teeth sparkled from the excellent care he gave them mostly because he dreaded the silence of a Dentist's office.

A personal question would drive him into a frenzy and his bell would clatter. He could not face knowing what he was.

Doc recalled that Hacke chose to live selectively. His residence was near an airport where thunderous jets roared by. To the north of his home was a 24-hour truck stop; to the south trains passed by his front window which he removed to intensify the noise.

Eventually, the noise became insufficient right after the rail line was discontinued, so he began to wander about with his bell, seeking louder noises. He avoided plants and sunsets, preferring fast moves. He favored careening sports cars and eating in gulps.

Doc strained to look down the corridor even though it was impossible. He missed the TV flicker. Also a meal, a wife to rub his poor, aching neck, a bunch of kids asking questions, a modern toilet and a chair to sit on.

That dreaded stomach growling was upon him. He had no pills to control the rumblings. He used what he had available, mind over matter. He concentrated on relaxing and imagined pleasant scenes, diverting his mind from the unseemly noises.

Doc waited until Hacke Cramm was asleep and all noises ceased and vowed he would triumph over indignity by morning.

Doc was right. Morning came. He was free, though still penned up. A beautiful toilet and wash basin, a fair view of the whole TV....and people...all this was coming. Though the amateurish and untrained were watching "The Killer" that night, he was suddenly in heaven, dwelling on all those classical grand marches, feeling justified if they stirringly extolled his triumph. He triumphed only because he was made to be a nothing.

He wailed for the correct moment of deliverance. It passed. Then he shrieked and shrieked. No one would slumber unless he triumphed. "Suicide," he shrieked; "Dead Man," he shrieked. He climbed the notches in that massive door barefooted until his toes cracked. Then in final resignation, he stood with his blanket over his head.

The shift changed. Doc sensed a soothing levitation, like dropping a 60 pound pack after a fifty mile hike.

Hal knocked.

Soon Doc was after his reserve of cigars which he secreted in the bottom drawer of the desk. Next he wanted his eye glasses, then his watch. He was reopening his senses to the influx of a renewed, resplendent life.

Behind he left his mark, "The Killer."

THE GREAT BLUE SIGN

Harvey Calsbeke finally had his choice words, elegant words which any person would appreciate hearing and, with the Mayor's assistance, evolved a practical means of displaying them for everyone to see at a glance.

On the day of the unveiling of the GREAT BLUE SIGN, Harvey left for Linden Avenue before sunrise to see it happen. He entered an apartment building across the street. He climbed two steps at a time. On the top floor he ascended a ladder to the roof.

Across the street from where Harvey stood the rays of the sun shown weakly upon the total surface of a canvass which was stretched across the broad expanse of a brick wall. He found the setting "perfect"

Seeing Harvey in position and noticing the wave of his arm, a man on the other building unfastened a rope. A gray canvass dropped.

"YOU ARE A WONDERFUL PERSON" were about the most exquisite words Harvey could think of saying to someone. Through the sign he would be speaking those beautiful words to many.

During a busier period, Harvey returned to observe his creation again.

Horns started honking as a huge crowd bulged out of Linden Avenue onto the town's main thoroughfare. Cars could not move for blocks in every direction, impeding traffic badly.

As Harvey approached the throng, he saw it was a human circle and something was going on at the core. He inched his way in and there, a young woman was sitting at a desk in the middle of the street, typing. Dangling from her neck was a stopwatch. Each time she glanced at the timepiece the crowd cried out, "faster." Harvey saw others performing. A dancer in a red ballerina skirt, two men chipping away with axes and an elderly man demonstrating his agility at hopscotch.

Harvey looked up at the sign. "No," this was not what he had in mind.. A "thank you," a kind word, that was all. Having them feel important, to have value....but this.-.this was a nightmare. Unwittingly he had resurrected a monster, a Roman Arena, a re-creation of Father Abe's restive dream where the lions had their way.

Harvey went to the street and asked, "What are you doing?"

"Performing."

"But why?'

"I can't be a wonderful person, until 1 prove it can 1? Like my dancing?"

Though the lady was wrinkled and flabby and had little poise or grace, Harvey nevertheless responded, " 1 like it"

The woman stopped dancing just then, but attributed it to fatigue. Accustomed to saying something only once, he never realized that he could have sent the woman off the street with another "I like it" or two.

Unfortunately, the group noticed the pause too. Being driven by the spirit of a loveless group mind they shouted again and again, "prove it," whereupon, with a fresh spurt of energy, the dancing continued.

Harvey observed that no thumbs were pointing down, not yet not while the proving energy which was being consumed on that spot was being applied to the thumb joints, keeping them from bending.

He had to hurry. His body became a ramrod as he thrust it directly at the crowd which surrounded him.

Harvey soon returned, again charging into the crowd. Three, six. nine; three, six, nine...he stretched his legs farther this time as he ran up the stairs to the roof of the same building where he stood but a few hours earlier.

From the rooftop he beheld the whole forest, sprawled out before him. He quickly placed a cone-shaped object to his mouth.

"You are deserving. You are deserving," he shouted downward..

The performers held back.

Five encircled people resumed their repetitious performance, but the tempo was perceptively slower.

Offering value without proof, Harvey shouted again, "You deserve the sign's meaning; you are worthy of it."

The actors were on a flat teeter totter, not up, not down but in between. They looked about, fearing a disapproving thumb.

"You don't get something for nothing," the crowd bellowed at the lonely sentinel perched overhead.

"You can't get water out of a bucket unless you fill it up first," shouted Harvey back at them...."and you can't give love if you haven't received it first"

"We must collect our love tax," they shouted at him.

"But you can't pay a love tax without love. First the love, then the tax," the lawyer debated. "You do deserve the meaning of the sign," he continued. "You arc likable. I like you," he cried with compassion.

It was unlike Harvey to be repeating himself. Yet the harmony within his soul appeared to confirm the legitimacy of his action. He appeared to be as one with Father Abe, the author of thoughts which once had no pertinence to him. With all his heart he could now believe them: "Just as the sun's repeated appearance is a blessing to us all, the repetition of the uncomplicated word is a blessing to the man who needs to hear it"

It was over. Every word uttered by Harvey had an identical meaning to whomever heard it. The generous, repetitious giving of value and importance had triumphed over the loveless demands of a sterile group mind.

There was no further performance, no hollow circle. The performers were no longer separated from the others but undifferentiated from them. Now. they too, have become members of the inescapable group mind. But they, the five, carried with them a love vaccine by which they became inoculated into believing what they truly were, WONDERFUL.

From behind him he heard, "Bravo! Bravo!"

It was Isidore, his head protruding from a hole in the roof.

"The Mayor and I got snarled up in the traffic jam you created here," he shouted "You are a public menace, you know?"

Harvey walked toward the head.

"You shouldn't be poppin' your head up from any hole, Isi. Somebody might take you for a prairie dog....then baaam."

"Funnnnyyy. Anything I can do for you?"

"Nope."

"Carry your horn?"

"Nope."

"Shouldn't you stick around in case somebody decides to do more dancing out there?"

"Nope."

"Self-sufficient son-of-a-bitch. aren't you?"

Both men stepped out of the building onto Linden Avenue. Suddenly, Isidore's demeanor became dead serious.

"The Mayor is waiting, Harve. We've got a problem.

"What?"

"It's Bullfinch...B.F. Bullfinch."

THE ORIGIN OF BULLFINCHTOWN

About a hundred years ago, in the Midwest, a town was in its earliest growth stages. About 400 settlers from the east settled in a valley close to a bend in the Missouri River. Two groups came into the area, one from the upper north and the other from the lower south. The wagon trails crisscrossed in the middle of the town. For a lack of any genuinely outstanding person within the settlement who could legitimately give the town a name, the Founding Fathers decided to call The Town "X," named for the shape of the wagon imprint.

As the town of X grew, communication with other towns and cities improved greatly. 'This created something of a problem. Not a big problem, but a definite inconvenience. You'd have to see it to believe it...like if you went to St. Louis for supplies and some stranger would ask, "Where you from partner?" You'd naturally say, "X"

"X who?" they'd ask and naturally you'd have to tell them the whole story. It happened that time would be a-wasting and if you didn't know the story right you'd hem and haw . There was a number of cowhands who got bushwhacked and done in by the Indians 'cause they stayed too long in one spot. When the plague settled in and riders went off to fetch help they naturally had to tell the name of the town.

They estimated the town would have had at least 10 more live ones if that confounded story wasn't told each time.

In the graveyard that sets far down by the cove there were 50 of them for sure, markers with a big "X" on them.

Still there was nobody famous enough in the town whose name could replace that abominable "X."

Some church person who decided that X was not only a hex but of the devil, recommended to the town Fathers that a famous person be created. If there was none in the town deserving enough, then they would make one.

It was on one early Spring morn that K.K. Bullfinch. B.F.'s Great Granddaddy and town Blacksmith, stepped forward at a critical meeting of the Town Board.

"I would like to become a 'famous' candidate." he proclaimed.

The critical-minded of the group complained that the name Bullfinch had no class. It sounded like a Zoo.

It has no nationality," others protested. "It isn't German, Irish or Italian...it isn't anything... but a zoo."

One more fault-finder was heard to say that he brought his horse to the stable for shoeing and K.K. put the shoe on the wrong hoof. "How can we use a name like Bullfinch." he complained. "He can't even put a shoe on the right hoof.'"

Some members of the Town Board were set on recommending Smith, Tom Smith, the grocer.

"What did he do famous?" others asked.

There was silence.

"But he's a friendly sort, says 'hello' and tips his hat to the ladies."

"And he doesn't shoe a horse on the wrong foot, either."

There was a good deal of wrangling in the Town Hall about renaming that frontier town, until the church person spoke out again.

"Let's have a duel...Smith versus Bullfinch."

Faces seemed to brighten as if they were just offered a solution...

"But what kind of duel, they asked?"

"Pistols," said the man with the wrongly shoed horse.

"The suggestion was made not without connivance. Smith was a marksman and R.R. Bullfinch could beat anyone in the town in arm wrestling but didn't know the difference between a bullet and his trigger finger.

Since the majority ruled, the decision was made in accordance with the suggestion of the church person, that there should be a duel. The weapons would not be arms as in arm wrestling, but pistols.

R.R. Bullfinch was given a choice as to location. The outcome would be final. Tomorrow the town would have a new name, either Smithtown or Bullfinchtown.

It was 7:30. A cold, brisk wind tugged at the thick wearing apparel of a group who stood huddled on a flat, an artificial terrain made of ice. The eye could sec emptiness for miles about as powdery snow was blown into a misty whiteness.

Two men separated from the group, each walking in opposite directions. The steps were slow, resisted by the wind and the desire to stay alive a moment longer. At ten paces each turned. The wind swirled furiously as both men took aim at each others anatomy.

A shot was heard, just one shot. Bullfinch missed.

Smith was down.

...This, of course, is the true story of how "X" Town became Bullfinchtown.

You may be interested in knowing that Tom Smith slipped on the ice, fell backwards and hit his head. The Town Board voted unanimously that they could not possibly have a town named after a man who couldn't remember his own name.

HERB THE VERB AND HIS MOM

The mother of Herb the Verb was startled by the clanging doors. As Doc Proud greeted her at Orkway's gate entrance she promptly reached into her purse and fumbled about with some difficulty, her right arm being immobilized in a sling. Before she spoke she handed Doc a picture.

'You look like my husband," she said.

The nose, the bald head, the round face, the big hairy ears, and the dimple in the chin were just about right, judged Doc.

Doc reminded the visitor that Herb was waiting.

She hesitated, explaining that he had embarrassed her on previous occasions.

Doc detected an asymmetry about the woman, one ear was stuffed with cotton. Doc noticed, and the other had dangling from it. a spherule of Black Hills Gold.

Doc guided the woman to a two-seater in a distant corner of the Day Hall. She sat down reluctantly as Herb entered upon the scene.

"Hub. bub, jub; moo. coo. too; Imm. dim, sim."

The mother's presence was bringing out the baby in Herb. He maintained his rhyming, but he seemed to have lost meaningful words.

"Tee, bee, gee; baa, la. gaa," were the best that Herb could do as he sat down next to his pudgy-faced relative. He immediately gave her check a pinch and took her by the hand. Then he began snuggling against her with greater fondness.

Once or twice she turned her cheek toward him, but he wanted a mouth kiss, which found her writhing and eventually sliding to the floor.

"Ub.dub, ub, dub, ub, nub dub."

Breathlessly she held Herb's head up with her unencumbered arm. Then the ordeal was over as Burt and Hal lifted Herb to a prone position and returned him to his previous lodging.

The mother brushed her hair back with the palm of her hand and invited Doc to search for the tiny bauble which adorned her ear.

Finally the lost was found and the mother settled back in a comfortable position. Before describing her husband to Doc Proud she wanted to be certain that Doc was not a relative.

Doc knew that the woman suffered at the hands of her husband and understood her caution.

"I wouldn't hurt you or Herb for anything in the world." he told her soothingly. "You are precious people."

She began to cry.

"He was all work," said the woman. "The community was a hunting ground for him. Herb was his prey. He would ferret him out of gymnasiums, baseball fields and pool halls or wherever kids hang out for relaxation, immobilize him with an arm lock and whisk him home to do work."

The mother's tears ceased, leaving behind a dark, reddened ring around her puffing eyes. She attempted to fasten her earring on with one hand hut her trembling fingers made the chore difficult. Doc moved to assist but held back, thinking any kind of kindness would only release more tears.

"It will be a matter of time before Herb's guilt makes him loving again," Doc reminded the mother. "In a little while, he'll stop blaming his dad and become a good boy again. In a week or two, if the pattern holds, he'll be home with you for Christmas. His rhyming will be gone, his baby talk will be gone and he'll be a responsible cheek-kisser."

"Thank you," said the mother with gratitude, wiping her moistening eyes.

She looked at her husband's picture again, took a careful look at Doc Proud, and asked, "Are you married?"

"We can poison him and I could take over his identity," Doc replied facetiously.

Let's work on that." said the mother, smiling for the first time.

With a worn out expression on her face she admitted. "I've never been happy being married to that scoundrel."

"You are not a wife but a dedicated protector, a referee, a buffer, who gets it from both ends."

In spite of Doc's analysis of her personality the Mother thought that he was "cute."

She heard that she was the nicest lady in the whole world from the Doctor and both of them left it at that. Then she fitted herself with a pair of dark glasses, stood up and carefully brushed the wrinkles in her dress.

Into the in-between zone, between one gate and the other, between the outside and inside of Orkway, walked a man with a black suit and white collar. Hal pressed the second red button and Father Abe entered the Day Hall. He removed a small bottle from a black leather case and proceeded to sprinkle its watery contents about. "Hello, father,"

"Why hello. Daniel...God bless you for your good work."

Thank you kindly...! See you received our message?"

"Yes, may I see him...He suffers terribly."

"Hal will help you. Father....incidentally, congratulations on your chairmanship . The Peace Committee selected a good man."

"Perhaps good, but hardly capable, Daniel. There is so much to learn."

Father paused, reached into his coat pocket and handed Doc a newspaper. "The committee divided the newspaper," he explained. Isidore Krasno had Honesty; Seth Culp and Harvey Calsbeke chose Value and Importance and my subject is Guilt, This is left...your assignment...Sports."

Doc was pleased...no, he was exhilarated. Sports was a passion for him. Whatever creative contributions he could make toward world peace he would do it watching sports. It was a perfect arrangement calling for a combination of duty and fun together.

"I accept," said Doc enthusiastically.. "But what shall 1 look for?" he asked.

"The love in Watergate. Look for the love in Watergate."

Doc Proud apologized to Herb the Verb's Mom who continued to wait patiently alone. Then he walked her to the clanging gates.

The Buzzz was heard followed by an inevitable clang and she stepped inside, Before the next Buzzz,-Clang she asked Doc, pointing at Father Abe, "Doesn't he look a little like my husband?"

ISIDORE'S PAINFUL DECISON

"It was necessary," Myra said, consoling Isidore as he agonized over his unhappy decision.

"She wanted me for her guardian because she had faith that I would keep her in her home forever. That look of abandonment when she was taken; it tore me up. The way she pleaded with me, Queenie. it made me......"."

"Made you cry?"

"Yeah, that too."

"That's why I love you, Darling. You have given me a big value, then you protected me like I was special. You have given Grandma Tillie a big value too."

"But I could not protect her. My wishes were not her wishes. God, that Home will kill her, Myra."

"We'll visit her and bring her things."

"Did you hear her say, 'I hate you, I hate you.' The pain of it made me turn away."

Surrounded by Myra's arms Isidore heard, "All that I am is devoted to you. All that I will ever be is yours for eternity. I forgive you."

Isidore looked into Myra's eyes ."My beloved," he said , "from now on I am proclaiming that I am not one but two. You can depend on a double kiss, a double hug and a double dose of 'I love you.' "

Finally the winds of affection gave way to the storms of rapture as the subject of Grandma Tillie Plover vanished, but only for a moment.

Just as the kissing ceased and Isidore was able to breath through his mouth again, he asked, "What happens in 8 months? Grandma has only $18,000 saved. At $2200 a month she has 8 months of caring at the "WE CARE" Nursing Home."

"What will happen then, precious?"

"Probably sell the house."

WHERE IS THE LOVE IN WATERGATE?

Where is the love in Watergate?

If a man is falling from the sky, what does he need to save him? If a man falls from power, what does he need to save him?

Nixon had his Watergate which tumbled him from the top, from power to no power. In the bat of an eyelash he fell from something to nothing; from greatness to mediocrity.

His net saved him. It wasn't the group mind, not Kissinger, not the people, not heads of state. It was one, two, perhaps, three who broke his fall. As he fell they embraced him; as he fell they cushioned him.

It didn't matter what he did. Only his being; only his person had meaning. He had more than any man could dream of...he had true love, conceived in the ethereal minds of the heavenly and nurtured in the gardens of family life.

In the Tomb Daniel Proud fell also, into the clutches of indignity. From integrity, pride and self respect he fell, as assuredly as did Nixon, as convincingly as if he fell without a parachute. The imprint on his brain gave him a memory which cushioned his fall. He knew that the net, a happier day, was awaiting him, to scoop him up safely.

The loyal family member proclaims innocence prior to any trial, freedom without justice, utilizing all forms of denial that, at all cost, the beloved will survive well. Meanwhile, the group mind is pleading for a sampling of the same loyal love that saved Nixon or Proud. Consider that media message, whether it involves news, lipstick, cars, or beer, it is a message of competition and struggle. No family could be cohesive with that message.

Indeed, the group mind procedures allow one to climb, the family procedures prepare to do the catching at the falling. If you have only the group mind formula and climb high and have no love net waiting below to enfold you when you fall, you are a pancake......

...Father Abe pondered these thoughts at home, even as he received word of Hacke Cramm's escape.

HACKE CRAMM'S ESCAPE

He went to have his brain's waves checked and they gave him a pill to fall asleep, not realizing he needed noise instead. Down two adjoining corridors Hacke fled with clumps of goop on his scalp, through a maze of tunnels which allowed traffic to flow underground in inclement weather, into the chapel, which was remotely situated near the far end of the golf course. Finally he busted a stained window.

His flight was the epitome of determination. Handcuffs, attached to a thick belt which girded his waist, glistened in the afternoon sun as he fled past hole eighteen through a raspberry thicket to an adjoining highway.

The temperature was below zero. Those silly, flimsy moccasins were left far behind, one on the church's altar, the other at the entrance of the tunnel. Barefooted, shackled and poorly clad, the Bellringer was gone. Thank goodness he had the whistling wind in his ears to give him succor.

The hunt for Hacke would be half-hearted. Disturbing the peace with noise was no great infraction. Society was prepared to tolerate his hard-won freedom providing he didn't turn up frozen like a popsicle inside a culvert

Doc was not present when Hacke Cramm eloped. A piece of paper had called him elsewhere. The messenger knocked on his door; the message insisting there was no greater importance except that he should drop everything else and come quickly two hundred and fifty miles to Wagner, to Court.

The procedural detail out of the way, Rachel and Harvey came together.
"We want to resuscitate the fallen sparrow in a Savage Wilderness," Harvey told Rachel.
"But who is the fallen sparrow?" she asked.
"Any person who is bad who deserves to be spat upon."
"And what is the Savage Wilderness?"
"That's the whole community doing the "spattering" by deriding, cajoling and accusing 'cause what they had seen done was bad."
"That person needs a kind word, but nobody will give it"
"Why?"
"'Cause he doesn't deserve it, that's why," said Harvey, convincingly. "But we've got to resuscitate that downed, trampled sparrow."
"What for? He's getting his just due. What about the people he hurt?"
"An eye-for-an-eye mentality is understandable, Rachel, but it is self-destructive. Bitterness is a flesh-and-soul cater. It is like the pollution which left on a wind yesterday returning on a wind tomorrow.....and then there is no peace."
Rachel wanted to know how students in her English class could help. "The students can practice their poetry writing skills in developing a greeting card...a card from the heart, a greeting with feeling, a message of value and importance," Harvey suggested.
"And then?" Rachel asked with a distinct curiosity.
"...And then the students check the current events and see what sparrow has fallen. The ego-building, esteem-enhancing message is sent..and the job is done....until the next sparrow falls.
Rachel wanted to know about the successes, the champs, the ones who go up skyward and do not fall down.
"They represent the second half to the Value and Importance School Project," Harvey explained. Rachel was surprised to learn that the winners received the same uplifting message as the fallen.
"If you are humiliated and at the bottom, you need to know that you continue to be important.. If you are on top, though your self esteem is high, you need to be encouraged to stay there. The message of the card is interpreted either way."
Rachel was excited for her students. In their project they could find that everyone needs a taste of V and 1, value and importance, and they, though inexperienced, have both the power and the opportunity to provide it.

Not two days had gone by before Harvey received a "V" and "I" creation, courtesy of Rachel Brink's English Class.
He read it and smiled. Then he read it again:

"I NEVER SAW ANYONE JUST LIKE YOU;
THERE CANNOT BE MANY, NOT EVEN A FEW.
THE MOLD THAT YOU CAME FROM HAD BROKEN IN TWO...
MY GOD, OH MERCY...YOU WONDERFUL YOU."

...then Harvey started whistling, "Zip a dee do dah, zip a dee day; My oh my, what a wonderful day..." because he felt good.

It was a five hour loss for Doc because the town did not have 12 healthy jurors. A flue epidemic postponed the court proceedings against a drunken burglar who wanted a warm place to sleep.

Five hours one way and five hours the other way, time Doc had no control over. Being born he was allotted just so many hours. How many times he stood in line or stopped for a light...that was time he gave also, time given to someone else so they could be first, for a moment. Doc recognized that giving others your time was also subtracting time from what you had left.

As Doc drove over and around sand hills, creeks and across vast expanses of flatlands, up and down Giant's Despair Mountain, toward Bullfinchtown, he remembered the 10 hours lost on the road and decided that, then and there, he would officially give the time to the judge, the accused drunk, and to the jury who was never selected. He would deduct that amount of time from the time he had left on earth and say that he did not give time, but love. Engaging himself with that thought he even began whistling a happy tune.

The following morning, Doc spoke with Orkway's high school "shrinks" and informed all three that they should look at him when he spoke. He informed all that the foible of the Bellringer's escape was not properly assessed.

No Guard rushed in for instant clarification or even self-accusation. Instead, Hal blamed Burt for not communicating to the pill-dispensing Physician that Hacke needed noise. But he thought it was Hal's job to inform him. "After all, his pay was 12 cents an hour more and he was the boss."

Hal was unable to deny the truth when he heard it. so his next logical move was to blame the food lift. It was stuck between floors.

Doc didn't even want to think how that was related, so he didn't bother asking. Instead, he looked at Len who sat straight out, with his body occupying a total of three chairs at once, balancing an apple on his abdomen.

Len reminded everyone that the chislic was ready for the "wigding" Christmas party at Vivian's.

"Wipe it out...celebration talk is inappropriate," claimed Doc with authority, lifting that piece of luscious fruit from its shaky perch and promptly opening his mouth like a hungry lion and biting it in half. That's how upset he was. Hacke's plight worried Doc, particularly since there weren't any noisy events scheduled in the town.

HARVE CALSBEKE'S VALUE AND IMPORTANCE PROJECT

Meanwhile, Harve Calsbeke was on the move again, implementing stage two of the "Value and Importance" project. He needed assistance from the children at the B.F. Bullfinch Public School, intermediate, District 3.

Schoolteacher and program coordinator Rachel Brink, who set high ideals for social awareness projects was consulted. Rachel had taken the matter up with the Committee on School Curricula who did not object to the propagation of Value and Importance. However they could not decide where it would fit. Would it be a new class? Where would it be taught and who would teach it?

With but a short deliberation, they decided that English should carry Value and Importance and the teacher most appropriate would be Rachel.

MERRY CHRISTMAS, THE SINGING DITTIES ARE HERE

The usual haul of Christmas cards, stuffed in his coat pocket. Doc entered his office. He pushed the papers back on his cluttered desk and formed a space big enough for a deflated basketball. A big envelope, one by two feet, was his primary target.

The phone rang.

Doc's eardrum was unexpectedly besieged by a string of hallelujahs following his first "hello." His second "hello" was a futile act.

He waited; then he heard Hal's voice: "Doc, the Blue Bells are here."

The Women's Barbershop Ditties were in the Day Hall. From the sound of the noise, all 40 of them were peeling out good cheer with vibrating tonsils.

"Be right over...damn complications."

Doc carried his gigantic envelope along, peeling it on his way. Heavy, wet snowflakes clung to his bare hands as he marched along briskly toward Orkway, examining one fat Christmas card. It came in pages, a quadruple-decker.

On the front, embossed in gold lettering, artistically displaying silver bells, was "MERRY CHRISTMAS."

On the second page, Angels were blowing slender horns?

On the third page was, "REJOICE, REJOICE AND A VERY, VERY MERRY CHRISTMAS with silver stars glittering on a black velvet background.

It was the loveliest card Doc had ever seen.

The true, generous spirit of Christmas was depicted in that one card as Doc stopped a moment to appreciate it. Thick snowflakes swirled about him.

On the fourth page he read,

"MERRY CHRISTMAS, I SAID;
THE OLD MAN IS DEAD.".....herb.

Doc stood at the steel gates. Above his head he remembered that archaic sign again, ALL YE WHO ENTER HERE ARE DOOMED FOREVER. Presently he wouldn't mind dooming the Ditties who were a pushy, overbearing bunch. Do-gooders, they'd squeeze into anywhere unsolicited and do their caterwauling even on a sleeting night.

But they sang magnificently in the bare corridors bereft of beauty. "Silent Night" was too. too touching to be interrupted by a "buzz-clang."

Hal noticed a handkerchief waving at him and hurried to the gates.

"How did they get in Hal?. Doc Proud, asked."

"Mostly by pushing."

"But the cells are empty. We sent the old man to the hospital for nutritional care. Didn't we?"

"We did"

"So they're singing to twenty empty cells?"

"Not quite."

The singing stopped; there was a double "Buzz-Clang" and Doc was in.

"Ariffa, Ariffa, Ariffa... how are you?"

"We're here as promised, Daniel, You know we wouldn't forget your crazy boys."

"You are an Angel... that's quite a treat you're giving my boys. They appreciate it to the depths of their Christian hearts....and your Ditties look great, slim and pretty."

Huge Ariffa giggled.

"Could we just say "Happy Yule" to the fruitcakes?"

Doc hesitated, then smiled approvingly, cupping one, pudgy, female hand into both of his.

"This way..."

The full bevy of forty Ditties surrounded Doc as he moved slowly down the corridor.

"There's one"

"He's cute."

"A fat, little Teddy Bear, ain't he."

That's how they described Len, who was occupying one of the cells. The Ditties moved back as Len approached the gate offering to give them his autograph..

Down the corridor further, they found it gratifying to huddle around Burt's cell. His red curly hair and freckles were the big attraction.

They call him a "poor boy, a misguided child, probably raised in an orphanage."

"What you in for, nice boy?" someone asked. About 80 ears were alerted for the reply.

"Strangling my wife with a garden hose.."

"Uggh," the sound of revulsion was heard in the crowd.

"It's all in the forehead...see how it slopes," someone surmised.

"I knew he was crazy; those cold eyes," another said.

"Ariffa, come here." came a yell from the end of the passageway.

Ariffa definitely wanted to see that one. With Doc at her side, she moved carefully, then looked inside cell 20.

"So this is the Mummy's Tomb."

FATHER ABE SEEKS A GUILTLESS PERSON

Father Abe would be offering a guilt expose to the Ministerial Society of Bullfinchtown. But first, he would require the assistance of two participants, one excessively guilty: the other guiltless.

Scrupulously guilty, Pamela Bullfinch would be perfect for half of his demonstrations.

In seeking an ideal, irresponsible person, Father found himself visiting B. F Bullfinch, owner and manager of the B.F. Bullfinch Marital Agency. It gave him an opportunity to eye the sinister Bull on his home turf.

The Bull had three daughters, Becky, Dolly and Pamela. Pamela was the oldest, living reclusively in a shabby corner of town.

Father expected lightening to strike again. He thought he might find another out of the same brood, a guiltless member. Getting the sanction of the Bull to use his children should be no problem. With Pamela in particular, he was generous. He had already promised all of her organs for scientific study.

Father Abe breathed a sigh of relief to see the insidious, notorious Bullfinch digging the first crop of spring dandelions in his front lawn. But he was an actor. To really know the man you would have to read about him at the town hall. Dandelion digging or not, he has an unscrupulous anti-social record a mile long.

The Bull was at home now, staid and controlled, without a whisper of meanness in his bones.

Becky, the youngest of the three daughters was at home, Father soon learned, but Dolly was elsewhere. She was looking for a white horse, having a fiery impulse to ride through Wounded Knee.

Inside the home father began witnessing a scuffle between a woman in a partially soaked bathrobe and a young girl in her teens.

"You're going to over-hydrate, Becky." the woman insisted, attempting to pull a jar of instant coffee from her hand. "It isn't good for your Epilepsy."

At the sound of Father's footsteps the mother turned suddenly, releasing the girl who was sitting on her prized can of coffee. The woman smiled faintly at the spectator, then attempted a motherly embrace. But Becky resisted, tucking her two feet squarely in the mother's abdomen and pushing hard, sending her reeling backwards.

The mother arose and, as quickly as a striking cobra, unfastened her bath robe, swished it overhead once, and smacked the fleeing girl across the legs with the heavy, wet portion, causing a moist, gushy noise. Without a sound, Becky scampered into her bedroom, clutching the prized jar of coffee to her chest. Meanwhile, the mother, holding her forearms across her unclad breasts fled with a swaying, dignified motion toward her bedroom.

"Bully-Boy, I'm dying," Father heard.

Busily chewing on some dried apricots during the ruckus, the Bull finally spoke: "Lana's choked off her breathing again. She's afraid of drowning in her own juices."

As routinely as if he did it 500 times, B.F. went to his wife. He propped her up against a pillow, took a round piece of wood, about four inches wide, from his back pocket and pried her mouth open. She was saved as soon as she bit down on the hickory.

Father couldn't possibly ask for additional cooperation from a family with such intense internal crises, so he left quietly.

As he approached his vehicle to leave, he heard hoof beats. The fifth member was bearing down on him riding a white horse. The ground shook. He flung himself on the ground as horse and rider sailed over car and human both. The stallion pivoted a quarter of a mile away.

Burnt rubber was the only remaining evidence of Father's visitation.

Continuing his search for a guiltless person, his itinerary called for a visit to Hacke Cramm's old flame, Mary Duffy, at her Camporee. She had an illegitimate son who could serve Father's purpose well.

On arriving at the trailer court, a band of motorcycle desperadoes were just leaving. Father couldn't help thinking as he watched them speed off. There could be one or two irresponsible ones in that bunch. Judging from the quantity of smoke they emitted, he was sure they weren't desperately interested in having a cup of coffee or a civil tete-a-tete.

Mrs. Duffy was examining her Airstream which stood in the center of her court. Only moments earlier she hid, having just emerged from a protective spot between her refrigerator and the side wall.

Deep, multiple scratches continued completely around the trailer "It's not the Duffy way," Mary cried out, as she looked angrily at the cycle tracks which surrounded the camper.

"Foxy...Foxy Duffy," she called, the sound of her strident voice reaching the ears of her 18 year old son.

Foxy Harold Duffy, lacking animation, walked slowly toward her.

"Call me, Maw?"

"You're improving a lot, just called you one time Foxy Harold. This trailer goes down by the grove for protection." she instructed. Then, raising her forefinger to heaven, she proclaimed, "It's the Duffy Way."

"Aw Maw, can't it wait, me and Mary......."

"I oughta take the bullwhip to your hide. Foxy Harold, messing with Mary Lou. I told you, when you copulate, you query about a hysterectomy first. If they got a full-blown hysterectomy they're safe for anything. Your Grandmaw had a hysterectomy at 21 and your maw had hers at 19. If anybody wants to fool with a Duffy, they do like the Duffies....

HARVEY'S WONDERFUL MESSAGE TO VIVIAN

The time was late. The streets were hollowing; the wailing sound of a police siren echoed in the deep recesses of Bullfinchtown as Father entered Vivian's place for a nightcap.

The premises were deserted. The college kids usually hung around evenings and, being Friday night, Father expected them to be jammed in Vivian's booths until midnight.

She barely noticed Father as he entered, cuddling her transistor close to her cheek as if it were an object of romance.

"Shush," she whispered, at the creaking of her guests shoes. "It's coming...here it comes."

Father arched over the counter, straining to hear what was coming.

"Heaven be praised." It was Harvey Calsbeke's voice, blessing everyone with, "You are a wonderful person." With her hand and her heart together, Vivian stood like a statue there before father.

"Nobody ever talked to me like that before," she said plaintively.

If only Harvey could see Vivian just then. One glimpse of that picture of rapture, that glorious feeling of appreciation, it would have compensated him for his Blue-sign fiasco many times over.

Vivian then set the alarm of her four-legged, antique time piece. The same public service announcement would be heard again, in 30 minutes.

Vivian was commending the Mayor for doing a wonderful job and offered "beers on the house" for three people, two present; one absent. Harvey was being offered a free beer but he wasn't around to drink it. Father settled for a diet root beer.

Vivian was blaming her empty establishment on a protest rally at the college.

"They want special courses or something," she said. "They want to study about "Mao-Tse-Tung, Witchcraft and Devil Worship"

Father crossed off the Bullfinch and Duffy samples of irresponsibility and decided to ask Vivian for her help....to recommend a truly irresponsible college student.

"Don't you have enough trouble, Father? People, as a rule, couldn't be happier if they never encountered one."

"Any simple dislike of another, destroys both a little," said Father, realizing he was adding a complexity to Vivian's mind which had only the minutest interest compared with Harvey's next midnight message.

THE PLIGHT OF TILLIE PLOVER

Tillie had a brother in Cincinnati who was being kept away by pressing business. When Ariffa was not picked to be guardian, she did some angry disowning. Being left out was an affront that ended the kinship on the spot. She vowed she would never speak to Tillie again and she was true to her word.

However she continued to be a loyal and protective aunt to Charlemagne and Zeph, Tillie's two bastard sons.

It was springtime and the crocus and the tulip were resurrecting into a state of majestic spender. Robins, blue jays, bobolinks, swallows, geese, and ducks were coming, being called by resolute instincts. This was the time for creativity to issue new life and the heavens would be overjoyed in the glory of it for, anything that had not been on this earth before, was being offered a chance.

Life was fresh; life was exquisite, thought Isidore, looking at the sunken, ashen face of an aged fireball. He could not tell if Grandma Tillie was listening. It was several weeks since she stroked his face and called him. "My son, Isi."

"The chances that you live, that you exist, are infinite," he told her. "How many sperms arc not you and how many unfertilized and fertilized eggs arc not you? What combination of two people coming together in a love bed are not you? There are myriads of combinations and finally...finally, you become you. With all those staggering odds against it, you live. You didn't ask to live, but you live."

With tears in his eyes. Isidore reached over and touched a hand which had touched him so caringly many times before.

"Grandma Tillie...Grandma Tillie," Isidore hesitated. "Thank you for having lived for me."

Tillie was Isidore's surrogate, replacing the mother he never knew. There were no legal ties, just fondness, closeness, caring and loving.

Tillie's antique dresser was in her room, her wheelchair too. Wheelchairs were forbidden in the corridors of the "We Care" Home for the Elderly. The rule was specific: "You walk the corridor or you leave."

Two separate piles of letters were on her dresser along with a burnt bra, a fresh quart of guava juice and a jewelry box containing bracelets, earrings, necklaces and three gold watches.

The bra was a memorabilia of by-gone days, found in the attic before the house was auctioned away. Queenie thought Tillie would enjoy the memories, including the stack of old letters found in her chest. These were letters from important people, political figures of that era, who were offering tribute to a dominant force in the area of women's rights.

When Tillie entered the "We Care" Home she was determined to get out She wrote letters, seeking reciprocation for earlier favors. The letters came back to the sender because Tillie's mind was living in the past. The white House was no longer the address of John F. Kennedy.

Lawyers, congressmen, governors, mayors....nobody came to her rescue. She felt abandoned.

When Tillie depended on the group mind, it did not respond; when she depended on her kin, her own did not respond either..

Isidore sat holding her hand. She was not speaking. She had stopped eating. The loveless group mind would say "She has a right to starve to death." But Isidore saw a woman and a young man caring for one another. It was personal...real personal. The group mind didn't have the capacity to understand that.

Isidore was bewildered. He was Guardian and his intervention was valid and legal. He consulted the Physician . "If she drank fluids, she would be all right," he was told.

In three days Isidore would make his decision.

He left Queenie behind with Tillie, needing to flee that setting common for its life- jolting decisions. Hoping to put his mind elsewhere, he headed Downtown to study labels.

PAMELA BULLFINCH NEEDED LOVE, NOT SEX

Living apart from her parents, with shades drawn both day and night, neighbors said Pamela Bullfinch was "crazy." When they saw her outdoors, it was always collecting discarded cigarettes in the street.

As a college student, it was men she collected. First, she collected love from men. Now, all the love in the world was condensed into the tip of a cigarette.

Pamela's condition did not evolve overnight, but there was one major incident, a final blow of personal devastation, which veered her life on its present course.

Several years ago, her friend Mary, who lived in a little, obscure rodeo town in the flatlands of Wyoming, was off to Kansas City again, this time to be with Pam.

Mary was a topless go-go dancer there once, sharing her room with two cabbies. Wild parties were frequent, a specialty of hers, which was meaningful only with older men in attendance.

Pam was seduced easily. Her grades declined rapidly as her sleeping habits became more irregular. She was indiscriminate, then pregnant.

Being cast off by the child's father, Pam began experiencing an excruciating guilt, after which she vowed never again to become involved with another man.

Soon Mary was employed with Pam as a cocktail waitress, meeting men at every turn. If Mary saw a handsome, well-dressed man, the older the better, she would turn to Pam and make known her desire to claim him for a lover. Men were lovers who she could please, yet degrade, simultaneously.

The older, more prominent family men were Mary's specialty because, when they fell, they would fall more deeply into the gutter of degradation. Like a diminutive group mind, Mary had power.. Mary had sex.

Some casual bar acquaintances had the word. Mary was planning a party. Pam was uninformed, but suspected something was in the wind as booze bottles began filling up the cupboards.

Finally, Pam protested.

"The place is too small, besides, you know how I feel about men after that guy left me holding a baby? It was hell. I don'l think sex is lo be given out all the time to anybody, Mary."

"Just to the man you love, Pam. Only him....then I love very easily."

"But don't you even get a guilty conscience about it?"

"I do. Excuse the word, when I "fuck"...then it's just a physical thing. I'm a lover, Pam. Not a "fucker.""

Mary was annoyed. Her long hair sweeping across her face, she yelled. "You keep your guilty conscience. I'm not like you and I don't think I like you."

Mary slammed the bedroom door behind her to be rid of Pam's overbearing attitude.

There it was, nice and naughty being separated temporarily by a slab of wood. How ghastly the struggle within one body if both of those opposing forces lurked in one person and there would be no door dividing them.

The relationship between the two girls suffered. For two days they barely tolerated each other....then Mary was gone, leaving behind some of her clothing and "Shalom," written on a note, stuffed in the neck of an empty Pepsi bottle.

It was the third night following that unyielding dialogue when Pam was awakened. Fists were pounding on the door. She was frightened at first. Peeking out the window through a flimsy curtain she saw, on the bright moonlit stairs, four or five figures.

This was the night of the party. Pam was sure of it.

They all appeared to be older men, Mary's specialty. One carried a pail, heaped with ice cubes.

Pam decided to wait quietly until they left. As she stood in the dark, un-stirring, she remembered the familiarity of this scene from her college days. Just then, for some unexplained reason, her mother came to mind. She was a fault-finding champion. In fact, finding fault was her definition of love.

Pamela could hear her mother saying, 'I wouldn't tell you how dumb you are if I didn't love you.'

Both of her parents practiced the rampant "NO," creating the unworthiness and rejection that throbbed within her pleading body. Feeling unwanted and hearing a whole bunch of fathers pounding as if they would shatter the door was too much to bear. She could never feel welcome on her father's lap. Now there were plenty of fathers within reach, tantalizing her, who would most generously give her their laps.

Pam barely realized that she was pacing the floor. She knew what she needed, love, not sex. The men at the door needed sex without love, being raised in a culture where the group mind says , "You don't get something for nothing." She realized sadly, that she could not have one without the other.

Her fiercely clutching hand uncorked a bottle. The liquid from it came too slowly. A brisk crack against the bed rail made it pour out. She swallowed and swallowed some more, until the bare floor was no longer cold to her feet. Her soaked pajamas were of no consequence. The door was the Alpha and Omega. Nothing else mattered on earth. The bottle broke, shattering on the floor, meaning nothing...only the door. Pamela unlatched it in three places and flung it open.

No one was there. Only the white gleaming stairs were visible in the moonlight.

For a half mile around a desperate, chilling voice could be heard, screaming in anguish, "Come back, come back."

Father Abe shuddered at Pam's agony, even as he sat in his car, across from her small, weed-encircled, curtained house. Looking very closely, he could see a pencil hole in each shade which was drawn full length over each window. Barbed cattle fencing had sagged out of sight in tall grass, giving the house an especially deserted look.

Father approached the unglamorous structure, carrying a pocket full of filter tips. He knocked, the whole house shuddering from the force of his rap.

As he waited, the pencil puncture in the shade covering the door window caught his eye. He held a filter up to the tiny peephole, whereupon the door creaked open quickly.

Pamela grasped the filter, squeezing it tightly. Before she could slam the door shut she spied a large handful of cigarette tips in Father's hand. Her eyes widened, like a well disciplined dog. she was willing to perform any act to acquire the symbolic love which Father held in his palm.

Father assessed the situation to be manageable as they drove off together. Pamela's reaching hand requiring the sustenance of a filter tip at intervals of five minutes. Father counted his filters, then he multiplied each by five. He could gain Pam's cooperation clear through the Ministerial meeting and have plenty of tips to return her home safely.

Ministers from all eighty churches were awaiting their arrival as they entered the place of fellowship of the Ministerial Society of Bulllinchtown.

Father and Pamela seated themselves at a large oval table.

As the murmuring settled into silence, Father rose and introduced his guest, "a prime example of one riddled with and immobilized by guilt." He described the conflict that tore at the soul of Pamela Bullfinch, then he apologized because he was unable to bring an irresponsible sort along.

When the priest was certain that his audience was fully attentive, he held up an invisible mirror and invited each to see himself by asking boldly: "What is our contribution to the mental state of Pamela Bullfinch?"

The reaction that followed generated defensiveness in that group in the same measure as a Boulder Dam would generate power. Suddenly, they were looking elsewhere, up, down, sideways...but not straight ahead. Those who whispered and laughed at the suggestion were skilled in expressing themselves in good taste.

Someone stood and proposed that he didn't even know Pamela and only God had the solution to her problem. Another emphasized her free will, that genuine, sincere prayer was the answer to her problem.

The problem lay in her upbringing, another advised. She required an abiding faith and desire to do the right things."

The mirror shattered. Father Abe's eminent colleagues made it clear...they could hurt nobody. Since they were driven constantly to be helping people, they could not see beyond the helping. Their good intentions appeared to them as everything. If they didn't intend to hurt...then they didn't hurt, they reasoned.

"Mere helping, what a pittance."' thought Father. He could not believe in the simplicity and convenience of that rationale since each and every one present had hurt others by his very existence. You didn't need a college degree in sadism; you can do it by eating too much. The excess food they ate, as evident by huge bellies, represented a deprivation of someone, somewhere.

Father could see the adamant single-mindedness of the group, defying him. They would deny hurting because they could not face a dose of Pamela's disease, guilt.

Unintentional hurting was as rampant as selfishness, Father explained. By knowing it, it was possible to avoid it. He who espoused the position that he could never hurt another was spewing a smoke screen. Under cover and, in the name of non-hurting, he could hurt insidiously and relentlessly.

Father then asked the group lo consider if their firm concern for God's word could be an escape, an alienation from the nature and needs of man.

"If our round pole does not fit into a square hole," he said, "it was not always that the square is not round enough...but possibly, the pole is not square enough."

It was a pity to hear again. "The word of God is the word of God, it can hurt no one."

Restively, Father held on to the table with both hands.

Suddenly, into the center of simmering discord, a terror struck.

"You son-of-a-bitch...God damn," Pamela shrieked, pummeling the table with two fists.

Quickly, Father forced a filter into her hand. She calmed down quickly but that unexpected outburst shook the pastors soundly.

They would question his good judgment privately, Father knew, but it would be orderly and scholarly in tone.

For the moment they were dividing anger into "just" and "unjust;" "reasonable" and "unreasonable.' Then they called it a "damnable passion, not to be expressed in the presence of man who is in the image of God, but to the cows and chickens who are lowly."

"Do as Abraham Lincoln did. Write down on a paper your swearing, then tear it up."

Pamela should have felt fortunate to be receiving special sermonizing, but her need was elsewhere.

Her hand was out again. Being more attentive, Father spied it immediately. He looked at his watch and noted, "Every two minutes."

Before Father could explain the necessity for an early departure to the group, there came a prickly summation from a remote voice: "It matters not how much man suffers as long as he is doing the will of God."

Pamela's hand was out again, trembling. She was being painfully torn by guilt. Now. what she took with her left hand, she gave back with her right. She was needing the symbolic love and simultaneously experiencing guilt for having it

"But she can't pay the love tax you demand," Father cried out. "She can't obey God."

Hurriedly, Pamela and Father left that unaccomodating group, totally dedicated to advice-giving...and little more.

Pamela was taken to a desk at the Southwest edge of town where persons usually came whose selfishness was denied them.

That mental hospital should have a new name. Father thought, as he drove away, an institution for Victims of the Rampant NO.

Coming to that ignominious place, Pamela's image was dropped into a cheap basket and called "second best."

Father asked himself. "What was the value of those relegated to the cheap basket "whether it was Foxy Duffy coming second to the Duffy tradition or Pamela Bullfinch coming second to doing the will of God? Surely the second best must have some value in a world where everyone yearns to be the BFST?"

WHY DO WINNERS WIN?

Pude, Chick. Groove, Doc Jr., and Stomach, all teenagers and all desperately involved in sports stood around looking awkward as Dad Proud laid out the plan.

They would observe a game and after a winner was determined, their job was to answer one question, "WHY did the winner win?"

Stomach thought it was "dumb" because he already knew why a team won. "They won because they crushed the other team." that's why.

"But what made them crush the other team?" Dad Proud asked.

"Dvorak. He shoots the ball; two seconds left. Score is 50 to 51. If he makes the basket, the Panthers win; if he misses. The Chicken Heads win."

"Good boy. Groove, "You've got it. Now, if somebody asks you. 'why did the Panthers win", you'd say?..."

"Dvorak got a lucky shot."

"Fantastic....probably if you asked 50 people at that game the same question, you might get the same answer from all."

Doc Jr. the 15 year old shy one asked. "You want us to ask 50 people?

"Yeah, yeah...do it.." said Dad Proud, thinking it would be an interesting experiment.

"What's in it for us?*' Pude asked, acting like every day was Christmas.

"I'll feed ya....you know people in Zimbabwe are starving?"

"That's stupid, commented Chick, "It isn't Zimbabwe. Dad, it's Ethiopia"

"I'm going to lose my girl friend unless I get better wheels." Pude pondered.

"Let's throw a few," said Chick, holding an official -sized football. "There's a fungus among us."

"I like you too," said the Daddy of them all who asked himself during quieter moments, "How do I know if I'm raising good kids or not?"

IN SEARCH OF A PEACEFUL SOCIETY

Back to a meeting, back to a sharing of minds, the Peace Committee came together to assess their gains, their losses and their in-betweens. The agenda included an updating on Value and Importance by Harvey Calsbeke. Honesty by Isidore Krasno and Guilt by Father Abe.

Given an hour of time for findings, opinions and discussions they each, in their own way, would proceed with new adventures on the pathway of a genuine peaceful society in Bullfinchtown.

Everything had gone smoothly, except Isidore hadn't shown up. According to the last report on his whereabouts, he had gone down town to check on businesses.

Two associates and helpers were identified. Harvey identified Rachel Brink as important in student and community education. Father Abe identified Doc Proud as an active and dedicated supporter of the project, then he reached down and lifted a rectangular object covered with a felt cloth. Allowing the cover to slip to the floor, he exposed a piece of artistry. There was a bunch of ordinary blue Concord grapes entitled "Family Love."

Underneath, it read..

"God brought as together to spark a relation
For love to increase and form a creation;
A cluster of grapes lo enjoy a new spring.
Begun with a promise and gold wedding ring."

A new direction was on father's mind. He had vowed to turn his fullest energies to that social unit which nurtured lives to give true love. Had he grown respectful? no....not respectful, actually he grew in awe of that place where close dependencies were valued and protected, the place where a father is needed to be a good father and a mother a good mother. His reference was the family, the indispensable factory of true love.

Father had delved into the lives of unhappy families and saw their fears. How desperately they concealed their selfish side, only to have it creep out disruptingly.

He wanted them to see their worse because, if it could never be seen, he knew it would forever linger to hurt and disrupt and ruin.

He described his playthings, "NICE" and "NAUGHTY." He discovered how the use of a "Nice" label could free a person to open the door a little to his hidden, naughty side.

The half-man needed to become a whole man because the half man could be only half known and, perhaps, dangerous. That process. Father knew, by inadvertently hurting others, would require mountains of trust to overcome. Then he lifted up his head courageously, defiantly. How worthwhile it all seemed; how infinitely worthwhile that people should become safer for each other by becoming aware of their totality.

The group recalled that it was Isidore, during his frequent excursions downtown to the business district, who made the ominous discovery that the half man existed not only in himself but as a universal contaminant.

It was in search of the hidden meanings of labels that he discovered the pompous manifestations of the half man. The glorious storefront enchantments which accompanied each piece of merchandise had the mark of the half man. Over and over the labels were demanding attention.

"I am first," They cried out like babes hungry for affection.

A shoe would never say, "I last for a couple of months; I peel here; I tear there; I crack in the sunshine." Because nobody would buy the shoe, the manufacturer would not say it either.

Information about the shoe is only half there because the maker is half there. Unfortunately, if he assumed his entirety, including honesty, both he and his shoe would be tossed in a cheap basket, becoming second rate.

It was clear to all, that the entire social system appeared to be based on a dishonesty game. It represented half men selling half truths. It gave rise to a strong word which was added to the lexicon of the Peace Committee: DECEPTION.

THE BULL HAS MET HIS MATCH

Seth Culp's secretary arrived with a message, "The Bull was agitating again."

The winter months held him at bay mostly because he feared frostbite. He could enter homes and pry out desirable members, but that was against his principles.

The Mayor stood up, his eyes blazing for battle.

"At all cost." he said, "B.F. must be stopped. Being tricky, he eluded us in the past. His surreptitious matchmaking is guided by greed, not peace..."

"But who would do the job?" Father asked.

The three men agreed that it would be someone who would not be taken in by the sinister Bull, whose specialty was finding long-suffering women for wealthy farmers and ranchers in outlying areas who needed someone to take for granted.

As far as the Peace Committee was concerned, the Bull's philosophy concerning marriage was not negotiable. While the Bull encouraged "living around," the Committee's unalterable viewpoint favored "living with." Though he sanctioned being single, though married, the Committee preferred being married with an emphasis on generating love.

The Bull believed that money made happiness but the Committee held steadfastly that love made happiness and happiness made love.

Standing erectly, the Major announced, "Our platform is clear. We have no sounder justification for acting decisively."

Just then the door opened and a breathless fourth member of the group staggered into the room, an entrance that startled everyone. He flung himself forcefully into the nearest vacant chair, exhausted, with just enough wind to request a bottle of alkaselzer.

"Queenie knocks a light off the GTO-Z.... says she was avoiding an accident." Isidore gasped. "She's a half hour late picking me up. What's the first thing she says, 'got a new vacuum" ..312 clams. A thousand times I told her. I could get one cheap. No, she don't want nobody else's vacuum in her house. 'New, new new,' she says. Everything she wants has to be bare-bottom, spanking new."

"Like to forge a check?" Harvey asked Isidore..."Would solve all your problems?"

Isidore said the question was "silly" and he didn't have time to fool around.

"Why not?" asked Mayor Seth Gulp.

"I got troubles enough. Don't need anymore."

At that very moment three quarters of the Peace Committee were satisfied. Indeed, they found a member who resisted complicating his life more. Selfishly, he was protecting his life from any further, corruptible influences.

"You win the prize, Isi," Father proclaimed.

"What prize?"

"Secret agent for the B.F. Bullfinch caper."

"Why me?"

"You passed the decency test... You're impeccably incorruptible."

"Geeze," Isidore responded., "all this recognition, just because a guy wants to stay out of trouble?"

He accepted the assignment but was not entirely pleased with the manner of presentation. He wanted more suspense...more thrill, a deep musical chord or two. with the message transmitted on an exploding tape.

Isidore wanted the others to know that there was a time limit to his commitment...three days.

The Four Musketeers raised their fists as a sign of pure backbone and shouted with one mind: "THE BULL HAS MET HIS MATCH."

RACHEL BRINK SEES A SPARROW FALLING

Sparrows were falling.

Rachel's English class responded to the news with additional creativity, intended to give value and importance to those who felt lowered in esteem. Already three pastors, one sheik, two millionaires, one sexual abuser, and three elected officials received the uplifting support of the young folk.

The class became alerted when another winged creature fell. The creativeness of the fresh young minds produced the touch, the feeling tone required for the best caring. Since the fallen had plummeted in Bullfinchtown itself, they decided to bring the message personally. In the tradition of pizza home deliveries it became the first Value Delivery Service in the world.

The elderly person was not eating when the group visited. She was leaning to one side in her wheel chair and was being fed soft food. She wouldn't swallow any. Instead, it lay in gobs on the floor, some barely hanging to the large barber's sheel which enshrouded her. Her eyes appeared lifeless, making no discernible contact with the friendly, smiling visitors.

"Tillie," one said, "Tillie."

Kneeling down and looking up into her empty eyes another said,

> "Tillie, though your mouth drools.
> And your lips quiver
> And your tongue gets in the way
> Of your mashed liver.
> Though your hand shakes
> And your body quakes
> And your cereal sits untouched.
> Don't die now, Tillie, don't die
> 'Cause there's nobody here to cry, Tillie,
> There's nobody here to cry.
> For many years you ate. Tillie;
> Tillie, don't stop now...
> Food is food and food is good.
> How can you forget that? How?
> Though your hand shakesAnd your body quakes
> And your cereal sits untouched.Don't die now, Tillie Plover. Don't die'Cause there's nobody here to cry, _
> There's nobody here to cry."

Briefly Tillie's eyes met, just for an instant, the eyes which pleadingly searched hers for a glimmer of life. There was a smile, a touch and the visit was over. Tillie Plover's eyelids drooped and she rested.

THE BULL AND HIS MARITAL AGENCY

The next day Isidore was on duty at his new assignment, observing B.F. Bullfinch at a distance as he enticed certain marriageable females into his trap.

"Be selfish with me, be selfish with me," he heard a blind man say as his cane bounded soundly along the curb.

A gray beard and dark glasses concealed B.F.'s identify'. For three hours. Isidore kept count of all the humiliation the Bull endured, including two kicks, five trips, four stomps on his toes, three chops on the neck. Sixteen times he was offered drugs with a one month supply of dirty needles, fourteen drinks of rubbing alcohol, and two poison rattlers.

It was pitiful for Isidore to see the Bull taking his work as a Marriage Broker so seriously, but that was his deviation, his trap. An unsuspecting victim, looking to be protective, would intervene. They usually did.

"Hey, cut that out," the Bull protested. Someone was helping him out of a gutter where he had landed from a karate chop to the loin.

"Can't you heed? Don't be kind." he chided. "Be selfish with me." he repeated, attempting to pull free of a sweet-scented, soft, helping hand.

^'Don'l you have a hat pin to jab me with? or a swift kick? "

"BUT I WASN'T RAISED THAT WAY."

"Well," said the Bull, showing off a sinister, wicked smile, "If you wasn't raised that way, then go ahead and care for me to yore li'l heart's content, baby."

"So that's his game." Isidore muttered as he watched the same woman scratch his
nose. Then, with her own comb, she was grooming his artificial beard. The more she was willing to do for the Bull, the more be expected. He had many marriageable prospects for that sort. It was the kind of woman that made his business lucrative. The farmers in outlying districts, especially those who had numerous chores to be done, would pay handsomely for such super-obedient women as did traveling business men who needed staunchly lonely wives.

Knowing what he knew about B.F. Bullfinch's operation, Isidore needed a Lib expert. A former student of the Tillie Plover School of Women's Rights, Rachel Brink was most suitable as a counter agent. A minister's wife, she played on the men's college football team some years back.

The most compellingly suitable requirement for the job. in Isidore's estimation, was the fact that male supremacy made Rachel's stomach turn.

Being considered for teaching the very first class in honesty to the 4th grade children, she treasured a memento or two from her college days. She saved twin towels, HIM and HIM and a lock of hair from her first Butch haircut.,

B.I,. Bullfinch looked for victims of the rampant NO, but not the Rachel Brink type, not those who demanded to be placed first. He preferred only those who could be treated as second best.

B.F. was an excellent a presentation of the GROUP MIND, taking advantage of the weaknesses in others, The women were certainly weakened by their second-best status and definitely more vulnerable to attack. Isidore was concerned about the intent of B.F. Did he wish to eradicate the second best from any assertive contention in life and relegate them to a permanent, inferior existence?

B.F. Bullfinch would be walking the streets again but first he treated his solicited aches and pains. His Marital Agency was the only one with massaging implements and bubbly-water bathing.

While healing himself, the Bullfinch Marital Agency, presenting a respectable front, would be arranging matches for the newly discovered street acquaintances who needed to please someone badly. Women who were intent on proving to a man that they loved him were worth their weight in gold...A minimum of $4,000 Bullfinch received for each order, his pains subsiding more and more with each transaction.

Unfortunately, the Bull's kind of woman wore out fast, but in getting to the door of the glue factory, she could raise five kids single-handedly, take care of a husband and provide for eight hired hands.

Bullfinch didn't care if they were loving—not as long as they were the doing kind. Being the doing kind, they were love seekers, constantly proving their worthiness to be loved. They were the kind who'd made a delicious meal; you'd sit down and slop it up, get up and burp, once or twice and have that woman standing there, not daring to demand a crumb of praise for her efforts because it might hurt your feelings. She tries harder the next time and the next, until she's ready for a trade-in.

"Because of the terrible reputation it gives to love factories, we've got to break the Bull's back." said Isidore, speaking to his accomplice, Rachel Brink, what was getting fighting mad as she listened to Isidore's briefing.

"Don't smile," he coached her. as both peered through a picket fence, attempting to catch sight of the elusive Bullfinch....."..and we don't want you looking happy, either."

Isidore pulled back, carefully looking Rachel over.

"Good," he whispered, glancing at her dress. It had that certain, correct, drab look, according to his specifications.

Noticing the absence of makeup on Rachel's face, he said, "Good. If he sees you liking frills, he'll figure you've got time to waste."

Isidore hearing a grinding sound, responded, "that surely wouldn't do, the Bull would pick that up immediately and abort his mission. If you must grit your teeth, keep your mouth shut...teeth-gritting means you're not sincere...and hold your head down, looking at the ground. He turns off seeing women who look proud...and when you walk, don't bounce, just maintain enough motion to keep you moving, .. nothing extra, that gives him the idea you're too free."

The weather conditions were excellent. The day was hot and humid, a dry parching wind blew loose grains of sand down necks, up noses and into unprotected eyes. It was a day which would heighten irritability in the most imperturbable of souls.

Crouching behind Isidore's GTO-Z, the two good guys soon heard the faint tapping of a cane and Bullfinches unfailing, self-destructive words, "Be selfish to me," coming toward them.

"Don't make a move 'til he's down." Isidore instructed Rachel.

That didn't take very long. Rachel saw the blind man stumble in the path of three young men. The first shoved him; the second cracked his glasses in two and the huskier of the three took a firm grip on his cane and whirled it around like a maypole, the bearded Bullfinch still hanging on.

"Be selfish to me," he continued to cry out as he lay bunched up in the shape of a question mark against a mail box.

Rachel moved in gently, compassionately and lifted the downed man to his feet.

The Bulls first words were predictable: "How were you raised, dear lady?"

"Doing for people." said Rachel, according to plan.

"Where's my glasses?" the Bull asked, squinting as he looked around.

Rachel held them in her hand...both pieces.

"Get me another pair, will you, honey, he asked her, testing the strength of her good upbringing.

Rachel responded immediately, turning to find another pair as the Bull's eyes brightened with satisfaction.

"Oh, Miss," he called to her...scrutinizing her faithfulness, "I'd like to take from an Indian best. When you get the glasses get a blanket and feather so's you'll look like a squaw."

When Rachel replied, "I will." the Bull snickered.

"...and, when you walk, walk pigeon-toed," he requested.

"I will." answered Rachel, gritting her teeth, but keeping her mouth shut.

B.F. was overjoyed as he awaited her return, thinking she would be ideal for a ranch.

Isidore's counter-trap was set, but why was Rachel feeling the steaming-hot, panting breath of a victorious Bullfinch on her neck? Perhaps it was because he never failed in his matchmaking antics before...and she knew it.

A woman approached the Bull dressed like a squaw and walking pigeon-toed. She was uneasy. Why didn't the Bull detect her trembling hands as she handed him the glasses? Did he see in her what he wanted to sec, what he also saw in the others? Since the Bull could only see her as a proving, pleasing woman, rather than a defiant one, he saw but one side of Rachel.

DOC IS VICTIMIZED

Doc devoted hours of his life jumping to the tune of a piece of paper. What made him particularly annoyed this time was the destination. It was the same as before. The town with the flu had gotten better so now they had enough jurors to try the drunk who fell asleep in a home.

Again the trip was nerve-wracking, two hundred and fify miles at a snail's pace in an eye-straining fog.

Il took 10 hours the first time. This time it would be impossible to return on the same day. When he finally got to his destination he was advised there would be no trial. The prisoner had escaped.

The next day, as soon as Daddy Proud set foot on the homestead again, something strange was happening. The kids wanted a family showdown. But Family

Government was Friday not Wednesday. Doc didn't even have the little envelopes with appropriate allowances in each prepared yet

Moose, who was Secretary, said chores were in a "sloppy state" and she couldn't keep track of who was doing what.

Chick was probably the instigator. He was almost like a Daddy when Daddy was away. After we sat down in the family room, Moose called the meeting to order.

"I got nothing to say," she said." "End of minutes."

"Well," said Chick, holding up Dad's King Edward cigars, "these have got to go." After crushing them in his bare hands, he immersed them in a pitcher of water and watched as the liquid turn light yellow, then a dirty brown.

"Smoking is not good for you, Dadio, so we're calling this here meeting to take a vote." proclaimed Moose. "I make a motion Dad stops smoking."

"Wait a minute," the Daddy of the house pleaded..."I've been smoking for 20 years...Have mercy on your poor Dad here. You know what happens to people who stop smoking? They get irritable. You wouldn't want a grouchy Dad would you?"

Nobody present was convinced by the argument, not even Mamolla. the Mother Hen of the brood.

"Then Dad's going to eat too much and get fat...and it will all be your fault."

The Secretary, looking about the Proud clan for further comments, tapped a coke bottle against the corner of a chair and announced, "Discussion is over, let's vote. Everybody in favor of bald-headed Dadolla stopping smoking raise your hands."

RACHEL BRINK TRIUMPHS

'Ihe next day. Rachel Brink strolled into the Bull's Den of Devisivcness, containing her trembling hand by clasping them together tightly.

"Ahhh. a nice lookin' filly. Open your mouth, woman, let's get a gander at yor teeth," greeted her as a tall, lean rancher with a huge cowboy hat pressed his thumb down on her chin.

Rachel's gritting teeth came in sight.

"Niiice, got good muscles on them bones, too."

As Rachel pulled away from the tight possessive grip of her purchaser, her stomach began to rumble. Courageously, she gripped the tall rancher's nose with one hand ...with the other, she yanked at his chin until the man opened his mouth.

"Ya oughtta git gold fillin's, yor rich enough. Aintcha?"

Bullfinch was beside himself. The worm never turned before.

"Where's your ranch, Tex'." Rachel continued, as her defiance swelled within her breast.

"Out yonder, a hundred mile."

"1 like big towns, Tex."

"Jest fifty-nine mile to Dry Gulch."

"How rich are ya,Tex?"

"Got bushels, woman."

"Then build me a town next door for right easy shoppin".

Need frilly dresses for all them swanky parties...no kids, no chores, two housemaids and a butler...jest faaaancy livin."   In a fit of rage Bullfinch tore off his false beard.

"Yor a perky one...ah do like that," said the rancher.

"Didn't know ya handled spunky ones. Bull. ..jes mah type... Hey, wait a second, precious." Rachel just escaped a bear hug . Lifting up her long dress that covered her ankles, she ran, fleeing the building.

"Get me 'nother, jes like her, Bull...pay ya double."

Bullfinch was in trouble. His entire operation would need revamping, but by no means was he stopped.

From that day on, the emphasis at the Bullfinch Marital Agency was changed from women proving their love to women who demanded respect.

ISIDORE AND QUEENIE VISIT TILLIE

Isidore was a bit more outgoing than the average man but he had the natural reserve of the universal male. He held within himself some private matters which he shared with only one person. To see him engrossed in the work of the moment, one could never tell what problem burdened his mind.

Queenie loved very much the man she chose for herself. The love he shared was a rare, rare love called responsibility. Queenie had a strong faith in his abilities ever since she saw him perform as an auctioneer. It was a delight to see his talent, to get the tongue working for him. rolling his R's, projecting his voice and that lovely move at the end of a sale. He would spin around as if it were in a sports meet, and would throw an imaginary discus. It was an endearing name between them, DISCUS, one Queenie used at special, personal moments.

She had used that name when the time approached where he, and none other, would decide about Tillie Plover and her eating problem.

Gingerly they were approaching the nursing station at the "We Care" Nursing home, seeking an update on Tillie's condition. The nurse looked into a chart for the latest documentation.

"Thank God. she ate something." blurted Queenie.

Isidore and Myra hurried to Tillie's-room. There she was. holding a magazine. She looked livelier.

There was smiling and greeting and hugging and tons of relief. For some reason, even Tillie's breathing was easier.

Then she pointed to her dresser. She wanted Queenie to have her jewelry.

"Charlesmagne gets half of everything." she said weakly, but he must stay single. Zeph gets the other half, but he must stay alive. Otherwise....otherwise everything goes to the Salvation Army.

Tillie looked at Isidore. "I don't know who is to blame why you are not my son. I love you the best.....you should have been my boy..."

THE ZEPHYR IS COMING

Fleetingly. like a sleek, black car with rusty blotches, the hearse moved through the night. Down the thoroughfare, it sped, making a screeching turn onto the grounds where in the remotest corner, stood Orkway, a stone protectorate of society.

That hearse could not have belonged to any reputable mortician. Twenty years old, it appeared resurrected from a junk yard, it was midnight and the Zephyr was being returned in style, with ample reclining room in the rear of his own vehicle.

The Zeph was a DWI and speeding. Before the policeman could check him out, he already slashed himself, then comfortably reclined where many cadavers had previously lay.

The process of rebirth in nature was happening but, as if to forfeit that exquisite metamorphosis, the Zephyr waited, clad only in white shorts, the garb of the numberless cell. If nature was about to bloom, the Zephyr would create a macabre scene to take the spotlight. If hearts would jump with joy over the passing of a constricting, frigid winter and would grow kinder in appreciation, the Zephyr would look the other way. There was ample time for tolerance, forgiveness, compassion. To act, is to act in the bloom of springtime, and act he did.

The blood-letter, pale as a snowflake. was Doc Proud's main adversary. He was destructing himself. His forearm was deformed, butchered into humps and ridges, and freshly bandaged.

They eyed each other, like two combatants, looking for weaknesses in their armor.

Attempting to make his grizzly appearance more tolerable, the Zephyr brought a Fez for Doc's bald head, the words spelled "Zef' backwards.

"My charges dropped yet?" Zeph asked. "I want the alcoholic treatment."

"We'll see...I'll find out." Doc replied ambiguously, appearing not to be too positively negative. It was those positive negatives, Doc knew, that could panic the Zephyr.

Doc cut a tiny bit of red tape in acquiring a few magazines on Alcoholism. He was relieved that the suicide-cell occupant was settling for that much, for the moment. Whatever was reasonable, Doc would surely provide.

"Give him what he wants." he advised Hal, "as long as he can't kill himself with it."

CONFESSIONS OF A PRIEST

What was it like to be a criminal and not care, to steal and not care? rather Abe's association with Doc brought him into a new dimention of experimentation with life. It brought him even further as he mused: "How would heaven be if it were completely normal-free?" When it came to stealing, the pure crazy were so opposite of the pure criminal. Would they steal? Absolutely not. Would they be mean? Absolutely not. Would they lie? Absolutely not Absolutely not they would not disobey their parents.

Father was half awake, yet dreaming. At last he was in heaven but on a puff of light cloud which was merely passing through, he noticed a tuft of hay on the road. A whole herd of cattle, a thousand, at least, were being driven out to that luscious mouthful of grass.

Floating along, Father noticed the sides of homes, quite open to view. Turning off the radio, one would turn off the main switch. Of course everything else would go dead. Thus, in heaven, radios played constantly or else nothing worked....and money, in its minted, printed form...was eaten.

"I'm here on an urgent matter...or two," Father asserted as he bolted through Doc Proud's office door. Quickly he sat down, but his sitting was uncomfortable. He wiggled, cleared his throat and jostled about seeking an idyllic nest for his posterior. His mannerisms, peculiar to the man. suddenly ceased. Then he relaxed and brushed his hand over his white collar.

"Look at my face?" he directed, as he stretched his neck toward Daniel Proud, his old chess buddy. "It was once smooth as the skin of a peach, now see how mismanaged it is?"

Doc rubbed his chin and adjusted his glasses for a closer look.

"Padre, friend....I've known you for years. Your face is no different."

"Well it is." Father insisted, rubbing the palms of his hands across his checks. "I've swore off shaving gels forever. In fact I threw mine away."

"You rushed down to tell me that?"

"I've come down to tell you that ...I'm a thief."

"Well, that's different. If you desire comradeship I'll introduce you to a few, not more than a stone's throw away, experts who would steal everything not riveted down,"

Doc shut the door completely. He sat back in his swivel chair.

"So, you stole a tube of shaving substance."

"Since the age of reason, I wouldn't dare."

Father was mopping his perspiring brow.

"But why now'.'"

"An adventure, an experiment; I don't know. Maybe knowing Hacke Cramm yanked me from my complacency. Dabbling in behavior of one sort or another, 1 decided to try a little deviancy, just to taste it, like experiencing a new food, or walking a new street. You understand..."

"Perfectly."

"Thanks, Daniel, I knew you would," said Father, heaving a deep sigh of relief. "Words just cannot adequately describe a man's sudden break with his ownuncompromising tradition. There is a progression of feelings, Daniel. Your insides are gushy. like you drank a quart of prune juice. It never happened before, but now everyone's eyes are upon you, only you, and the fear of having a hand drop accusingly on your shoulder drives you to the edge. Finally you are outside, your tube of gel in your pocket. You look back and nobody is pursuing you. You take a deep breath because you are free...you have succeeded in defying the code, the ten commandments, all that you have ever been taught. You want to break loose...you want to go to an isolated hill somewhere to scream it out, 'I've done it,' and then you begin to feel it was easy, too easy. 'I can do it again,' you say...but it is only words, Now you will think about it, and the more you think the more your past chases you and corners you and shakes a finger at you. Then, what you stole turns sour."

"Words right out of my mouth, Father."

"You mean, you..."

"Yep, did the same. We can organize our own chapter of Thieves Anonymous, Father."

"I sure thank you for liking me anyway, Daniel."

"Liking a person anyway is where the love action is."

"Both men smiled at each other.

"Glad you brought your collar along. Maybe you can help me prepare for a funeral."

"Somebody die?"

"Nope"

ENTER, THE MAYOR OF LITTLEFIELD

Doc entered the Grand Chamber, the Day Hall on Orkway. He walked briskly, followed by a priest, without the slightest notice of the two figures viewing a home movie.

Reviving the early run years of his life, the Zephyr's uncle came to "booster up" the disconsolate spirit of the ashen-skinned man sitting nearby, gently scratching his healing arm.

Doc quickly glanced at the four empty slots on the chalk board in the main office. Soon there would be more than enough bodies and the Mummy's Tomb would be in demand once more, Doc thought, vowing to double up before he went that course. He reached down and peeled away several laundry forms, rolled them up into a cylinder and gently bopped Hal, seated at the desk, on the head.

"We're almost full," he said. "Now you're earning your money."

"Yeah, we're thinking of starling a loan company, Doc," Hal retorted dryly.

Doc approached the two men in the Day hall and introduced himself to the older, gray-haired gentleman and thanked him for coming.

Little more was being said as the sound of the projector and sight of images on the wall occupied the onlookers.

The scenes were in color, portraying a summer time of fun. There was the Zeph, not more than 8 or 9, riding his first bicycle. Then the scene changes to a cabin at a lake and boating.

Doc stood aside with Father as he looked as Zeph for any discernible reactions. So far he sat pensively, his hand folded, his two thumbs, supporting his chin, and his two pinkies stuck in the orifices of his nose. He sat through the scenes of people picnicking, playing badminton in a back yard, cooking steaks on a backyard grill...

Then a room came in view. It was the Zeph's sleeping quarters of many years ago. His eyes seemed to moisten at the sight of the crib, of a bed. and finally a door.

He stood up slowly, then a remarkable sort of posturing occurred. The Zeph was bending over, way over. Though his body was as straight as a board, he was pitched forward, as if an invisible cord were holding him back. It was a remarkable fete. Whatever it meant, it was soon over, just as the movie scene changed.

As the Zeph was adjusting his two-penny state slippers, Doc saw his chance. He quickly unraveled his paper, moved to the Zephyr's side, pressed his ball-point and gave it to the young man to sign.

If he signed that sheet he would be receiving, personally, whatever laundry items might be listed.

He signed it.

Just as the Zeph began to stretch out comfortably in his chair Doc presented another laundry form for signing.

"This one is for your eyes," he said. "The other one was for your kidneys. After you're dead, the Medical School gets your body parts. Sign here."

"What did I do to you?" came a sullen reply, peppered with irritation.

Doc ambled across the floor about ten feet to pick up his pen where the Zephyr flung it.

Dying was not a palatable subject for the uncle who quickly pulled the projector back, enlarging the wall image.

Father looked closely at the projectionist. "I know that man," he told Doc quietly. "The Mayor of Littlefield."

"Oh boy, a politician," reacted Doc. "He'll never understand."

"I'll fix it," father reassured him, as he strolled casually over to the older gentleman.

Meanwhile, Doc headed for the station, peeking intermittently at the figures he left behind.

The man with the gray shirt started shaking his head. If Doc could read non-verbal cues, it was 'No, No, No' over and over.

Then the projector ran out of film.

What happened next. Doc couldn't believe. The two conversing men began to sing together, "Rock of Ages." That was the pre-selected hymn for the Zephyr's funeral.

Father next invited the Zephyr to stand up for a measuring, for the coffin. He stood up...but only for the purpose of retreating hastily to cell unnumbered. He pulled the gate behind him, calmly lay down on the mattress and began reading about alcoholism.

Doc rushed out to meet the Mayor of Littlefield again only to learn that his massive load of negative signals represented a bad nervous tick which was exacerbated by the subject of death.

The politician was interested in getting the charges dropped for his nephew and Doc supported the same position enthusiastically.

The Mayor busied himself with packaging his movie equipment, but Doc could not have him leave without learning more about Zeph's slant.

"It goes far back,' he explained. "My sister-in law, his mother, Tillie Plover, liked to visit the neighbors, being a gossip and outgoing and enjoying coffee with friends she had her routine well-mapped out. 1 don't know if her leaving him behind started it, but the boy began throwing everything in sight She swore she would go crazy if she didn't get out of that house.

Well," continued the Mayor, "there was nothing wrong with that except she couldn't take him along. She didn't believe in baby sitters because, you know, they didn't make good mothers. She used to say, 'An instinct for motherin' was a thousand times in the better than a hired woman.'"

"....and then...?" Doc asked.

"So she couldn't' take the boy and she didn't believe in having him watched so she then did the right best thing she knew of. She haltered him. For weeks he was just out of reach of that doorknob. He tried to bend over whichever way, but he'd never touch it."

"So. that's how he learned to bend over at that fantastic angle."

"That's the story as best as I can piece it together. Doctor."

The politician looked at his watch.

"Got lo scoot. Got to visit a body here in Bullfinchtown about getting the boy out."

Before leaving, the major of Littlefield passed his card around. He was running for Governor.

THE CELL UN-NUMBERED

The next day. Doc Proud stood in front of the cell without a number.

"These yours?" he asked, holding up a pair of thick, cotton socks that were prematurely returned from the laundry.

Zeph shrugged one shoulder.

Doc spelled a name stamped on the inside, "P-L-0-V-E-R"

"That your name?"

The person addressed brushed the Newsweek from his cot, lifted his feet off the floor, swiveled around, stretched, lay face up and snapped his eyes shut.

"These yours?" Doc asked again. But now he was displaying two double-edged razor blades.

Not a word came from the lips of the suicide man; there was dead silence.

Doc was looking at a classical, professional masochist who was dedicated lo achieving lifelessness.

"Life is exquisite." he implored, speaking to a cot with a lump on it "Life is beauty, a fly with many eyes to see many sunrises at once, the clear, crisp mornings with traces of the first snow in the crevices of the plowed fields; the warm meadows, the fresh fruits that give life to the tasting sense; the scented flowers that give vitality to the smelling sense. The harmony of nature coming can make living a happy, wonderful experience.

Out of myriad's of complexities you've arrived. You live...as special as the sky is blue are you, Zeph...you live."

The eyes opened. The body moved abruptly.

Looking directly at Doc Proud, the Zephyr demanded his rights. He wanted his personal property back.

THE HONESTY TAX

A means of communication was needed to carry information from the hallowed meeting place of the Peace Committee to the citizens of Bullfinch Town. That vehicle was the Peace Gazette.

The very first article dealt with a controversial approach in selling...For example,
words connoting permanence as "will always treat you right," and by calling you by your Christian name and they hardly know you as, "Joe...how are you?"

They call you Joe if it helps them to get your money. If they don't succeed, then they don't care if your name is Blehovnek. The Committee says, "It is unfair to cozy up to human feelings and try to make a buck out of it."

The Peace Committee decided it would be sacrilegious to use words manufactured in the Family's love factory and have them applied to the connivance of the group mind. To refer to a car as "something good enough to go to bed with" or to call it a "Sweetheart" was unforgivable.

To say you get a free tire if you buy a car is reasonable. However, to say you get a free tire as if no strings are attached and propagate the fundamental belief that you don't get something for nothing is a scurrilous contradiction that purveys a fundamental dishonesty.

"If the group mind uses deceptiveness as a ploy to make money, it should pay anhonesty tax." Therefore, all unacceptable mockery of dignified conduct, when used in the pursuit of profit, should be taxed.

As for shopping hints, watch out for pre-packaged fruits and vegetables. If fruits are rotten, sour, or moldy, return promptly. Also, watch out for the misting trap, squirting water on vegetables trying to make old ones look fresh. Always check the bottom of the pile for a better pick of fruits and please do not buy any pork, bacon, or lard that is labeled cholesterol-free.

WHY DID THE PANTHERS WIN?

The game was over. The vanquishers were jumping up and down, hugging each other. They won their division.

"It was good coaching that did it," said Pude. .

"It was the new defensive strategy," said Groove.

"The family support did it...home court," said Doc. Jr.

"No way " said Stomach, "it was Stepanick's 22 points."

Chick thought it was the turnovers and the extra day of practice that won the game.

"So why did they win?" asked their Dad Just after feasting on a chicken dinner with stuffing and cranberry sauce and pumpkin pie.

"We just told you, dad, weren't you listening," Chick pointed out

"Yeah, we don't chew our chicken twice," Groove remarked, cynically. "Heh. heh. heh."

"But listen..." Dad Proud tried to get Doc from threatening Stomach with a fork.

"Groove is hiding beer in the closet," snitched Moose.

"All cans of beer belong in the refrigerator." Dad announced. "Beer tastes better cold.'

"Hey, what about Playboy...Does that go in the refrigerator too. Dad?"

"No, Doc, you can keep that hidden under your pillow."

"Pude," Dad Proud said aloud, hoping to resume an earlier discussion, "You said it was good coaching that made the Panthers win. Groove thought it was good defense. Everybody had a different answer."

"C'mon. Dad, get the marbles out. Get to the point," said Chick. "You talk like an old fogy."

"Glad you asked, son...it's like this... if you take away any one of them reasons for winning, I mean, just subtract them, like they never happened....."

"Then what?"

"Could the Panthers have won anyway? Could they have won if they played away, instead of at home? Could they have won if Stepanik didn't make 22 points?"

"That's stupid, dad," said Stomach, "sure they could have won...something else could have happened."

"Congratulations, that's good logic, son."

"Now, who knows why the Panthers won? There is one irrefutable answer.'"

"One what?"

"Irrefutable. It's in the dictionary, Doc."

"Let me ask again... Who at this table knows why the Panthers won... positively?"

The group of adolescent minds were thinking...

"Give up?"

Nobody wanted to give up.

"They won because the Chicken Heads lost," said Chick finally.

"Great...you've got it. It was impossible for the winner to win properly unless the loser lost"

Winning over or triumphing, that was the direction of progress. What would life be like if there were no inferior shoes. There would be no better shoes. What would it be like if there were no loser? There would be no winners.

Since they could not discern any further purpose for their continued presence, the kids just "flaked off."

Pude was on for dishes. Mother Cora Proud sat down for a bit of listening. Whether she did it out of genuine interest or duty, it didn't matter. She was a compliant servant of nature, filling a vacuum around the kitchen table. Besides, she gave her attention to special ears, big ones like Daniel's.

As she twirled a dish cloth between her fingers, batted her eyelashes flirtatiously and placed her hands under her chin like a warm, empathic listener, she listened:

"Wherever there is a best, there is a second best." said her husband. "Every moment we live is a second best moment to the one that replaces it. Every NOW moment is the very best that the whole universe has to offer. In a moment more, it will be second best.

Our wish is to give our children a better chance, better than our own," said Daniel, winking at his wife. What else? It is common sense but only because it is a rule of nature.

Who are the winners? The children. And who are the second best? The parents." Mother Proud looked at a small kitchen clock that worked on a single battery. The dishes weren't done. She could sec Pude catching a football through the kitchen window and left to call him.

THE CHALLENGE OF HACKE CRAMM

Two men walked together in the twilight hours in a flower carpeted orchard behind Doc Proud's giant brick house and listened to the "caw- caw" of crows perched on a nearby grainery as warm winds wafted through the flatlands.

St. Michael gave value to man," Daniel. "The freedom he gave was not given to a shoe, but to a man. A shoe won't change, but man will. To do better, a shoe needs another shoe. For man to do better, he doesn't need replacement. He needs an alteration from within. As a man, I want to help him, but Hacke is so serious, Daniel. 1 absolutely could say nothing to change the man's mind. He was beyond reason."

"Reason is a luxury," said Doc Proud, brushing his shoe against stems of wildflowers, "but only for those without need. With need you disengage reason and divorce principle. There is one guide, Padre, when the prickly thorn is painful, yank it out."

"But 1 stood with him and felt his tremor, though I was calm and warm. 1 sat with him and he couldn't stand the inaction. I ate with him and he swallowed his food massively, choking at every bite."

Tucking his hands under his armpits, Father Abe declared despairingly," 1 was a helpless cork in the maelstrom of one sick life. 1 whirled endlessly, not knowing where to grab, what to call a beginning, or how to act."

Pointing to a cherry tree, Father stated, "I can trim this piece of nature's creation. I can horticulture this whole acre, Dan." He reached down for a stone. "I can even hold this up and observe it being done and I am pleased that I can do it but, for Hacke, I have zero merit; I have minus meaning. I shudder at the thought of my helplessness."

"You're involved. Padre, maybe too involved."

Father laughed. He held back for a mere instant then he asked, "What do I do?"

Doc braced himself against the trunk of a Bartlet Pear and asked Father very frankly if he had years to sacrifice for one "misfit" He advised him, as a friend, to return to his normal flock and bask in the luxury of all those truths that were spelled out for him as a child.

"Play with normals," Doc said emphatically. "They're your style."

I'm switching for Hacke," Father said resolutely. "Now tell me how I help, or do I go to a book?"

"Look here. Padre," Doc replied, stopping suddenly, and pointing. "What if you chew Hacke up like the rabbits have done to his young tree. It may not live."

Doc noticed that his priest started to pout. It was a childish mechanism, a struggle lost on the battlefield of a quaint probably universal regression where hurting is done without speaking.

"If he would not speak, I would," decided Doc.

"You can do it," he said, reversing himself instantly.

The words were magic, lather's more stable, normal habits had been revived on the spot as his head raised to its normal height.

"Don't help Hacke, rather give to him," Doc instructed. "When you help you provide what you can afford, like an extra dollar; when you give it means you provide what you yourself need. Can you do that?"

"Certainly."

"Now don't be afraid." Doc continued "Fear is contagious."

The two men walked toward the house and some hot coffee that awaited them.

'Moderation is a rule of nature. It is the in-between position that great things are accomplished. Remember, Father, no plant survives on the moon; no mind functions well at extremes and...be truthful, but know that in truth there can be the most torturous pain....and remember, Hacke is but half normal. He is not all there. When he is total, he will be well.".

Father listened attentively.

"And to get him total you must accommodate his needs."

As the two men approached the front steps. Pude was there.

"Coffee's ready, folks."

"Thanks, son, we'll be right in."

Doc turned to his friend. "Remember, love in hard times counts most. Hacke will test your love thoroughly. A word of caution: if your love-giving is about to bankrupt you and you feel drained and empty...stop, run. Save yourself. "

Father reached very deep down into his coat pocket and pulled out Hacke's old bell.

"He'd want you to have it. Doc."

It seemed like a good idea, to collect those mementos of the old pros. The Zephyr's razor blades were at the station in some cupboard and Herb the Verb's lovely Christmas Card was filed in a drawer under miscellaneous.

Finally, before entering the large mansion-like brick dwelling, Doc reminded his dedicated student that the cause of Hacke's condition was in his brain. "Thought you should know that Hacke's choice treatment could be BRAIN REPLACEMENT."

THE MAYOR OF LITTLEFIELD AND ARIFFA CONFER

The Mayor of Littlefield had an opportunity to meet with a member of the fairer sex during his last visit with the Zephyr. It was his chocolate-eating sister, Ariffa, who filled him in on the more private, socially unannounced procedures at the Orkway facility. The Mummy's Tomb was one of those procedures. But it was the potty that just rubbed Ariffa the wrong way. There was none.

There was a hidden motive why Ariffa and her Ditties invited themselves. Arriffa wanted to see cell 20.

Charlesmagne Plover, called Ziggy, 'cause he couldn't pronounce his first name, got a message to Arriffa. She was his aunt and he was vindictive. He was mad at the one he "woved" for putting him in the Tomb.

While Arriffa described the Mummy's Tomb the Mayor of Littlefield became angry, but, being a professional politician looking to high office, he was becoming expert at using anger constructively. He was thinking of the changes he would make when he became Governor.

"...And they wanted to bury Zeph alive," he told Ariffa. "Instead of feeling sorry for him, like they should, they were getting him ready for the cemetery."

'The Mayor's neck began to twitch as Ariffa's faced flushed red with indignation. She reached into her purse. Clutching three chocolates in her hand, she plugged her mouth instantly.

Meanwhile, several other persons, sitting in the same, small restaurant saw the Mayor violently disagreeing with a woman. It was the mention of death that made him do it, manifesting that uncontrollable head twitch which communicate clearly, over and over a very positive "NO."

It was fortunate the Mayor of Littlefield was not at the "WE CARE" Nursing Home today. His twitch would have been so out of control his head would practically come off. In that place a close relative had just died.

THE MEANING OF KNOE

It was during the time of the referendum that Isidore received word of Grandma Tillie's death. Amidst the voters at the local precinct he hid his face and wept. Bumping into several people he sought privacy for his grief-stricken, uncoordinated body. Finally, he stumbled into a corner.

In the throes of sorrow, Isidore stood alone, unnoticed as the world turned. The Democratic process, the voting, the tallying continued.

That evening, the results were in.

Hullfinchtown had a new name," Seth Gulp proclaimed, standing on the steps of the courthouse.

"Be it known, from this day on, that our town be called KNOE."

Crowds danced about on the street as fireworks flashed in the evening sky near the cove. Rachel Brink was thankful because Knoe was no General. Knoe was not a Governor either or any great man.

Knoe was an attitude. It meant the same as NO. In fact, on the ballot the voter's choice was between Bullfinchtown or No Bullfinchtown. 'No Bullfinchtown won. "No" won. ...and what is the significance? If someone is giving you drugs you say, "NO."

Knoe meant to be assertive. It meant, don't whimper. If you have rights, defend them. Let no man be rewarded for cheating you. It meant, speak out how you feel.

Knoe meant to defy, but to defy responsibly. It meant not to resist conformity but to add to conformity another alternative,

Knoe meant to be yourself...it meant to think for yourself. Knoe meant to respect and love yourself.

A SPARROW HAD PLUMMETED

Before passing on, Grandma Tillic asked for Isi. She told him she had one regret, that he was not her child.

In keeping with events, Rachel Brink called for a literary emergency. A sparrow had plummeted and her English class was placed on notice to offer Value and Importance.

To a dead person?" they questioned. They had never done it for the deceased, besides, "a dead person can't appreciate it," the students reasoned. Their self esteem couldn't get cranked up any higher and they couldn't feel any more important.

"To their spirit...tell it to their spirit." suggested Rachel. "Pretend it's still around."

"WHO DEPARTS IS NEVER GONE," she wrote on the chalk board.

In not less than five hours of rhyming and composition the students finished with eight lovely lines of emulation.

WHO DEPARTS IS NEVER GONE,

THERE IS NO PLACE FOR DOUBT..
NOW YOU SEE THAT LOVELY SOUL
IN MANY FORMS ABOUT.
THE HILLS AND VALLEYS BOTH PROCLAIM
MANKIND SHALL NEVER BE THE SAME...
OUR LORD IS PLEASED, REJOICE TODAY,
A GOOD, GOOD SHEPHERD PASSED THIS WAY. „

The reading was synchronized. All 25 students read the tribute to the fallen sparrow together.

A moment of silence followed.

A piece of chalk fell to the floor.

Everyone present knew. The spirit of Tillie Plover just said, "TIIANK YOU

THE INSPIRING INFLUENCE OF ST. MICHAEL

St Michael was honored in the school system of Knoe. Here was a leader who looked to nature for guidance. He followed the stream and did not rebel. He did not cut here, trim mere; meander here, dam up there. He moved with smoothness, as the weaving stream did flow.

His children were stifled, bound, contained, box in by a disciplining authority. He looked at the repressive powers, the unrestrained forces which cut across, gauging new riverbeds with wars, trauma and pain of body and spirit and saw in it the folly of resisting the wisdom of nature.

Nature spoke and said, "if a person has anguish, he needs accommodation. St Michael spoke, "if a person cries out for freedom, he should have it" Nature said, "man must be allowed to grow, but not with a burlap covering his head." St. Michael provided that man be enriched in knowledge so he can generate a complete growth of intellect. Nature said, "man must be permitted to have choice; without choice man was incomplete;" St. Michael announced that man will grow with options so that he will become both straight and tall.

Nature said, man must be given love to become full-grown; St Michael decided that giving love meant giving of one's own need. To his flock he gave understanding. He entered into the inner chambers of their hearts and saw the turmoil and said, indeed there was suffering. He looked into their eyes and saw the pleading and knew instantly that a rule of nature had been abused, that man is at his best if not driven to an extreme. He saw them begging to be significant and immediately gave them an importance exceeding their expectations. Then they began to move, to gyrate, to change and, seeing the gain in it, he gave them blessing to continue.

It took many years and horrible wars to bring the nations of the world into line. It took weeks and months to bring it all down to nothingness, even without war. St. Michael did not have his armies pitted against armies; he had the most powerful force in the universe on his side. He quietly looked at the need in the hearts of men and allowed its fulfillment

St. Michael was a good parent and good model for the children to emulate. He wanted his children to be the best and himself second best. The second best with power were the saintly because they encouraged others to the front, to the best position. But the best with power had no concern for anyone but themselves, being concerned with maintaining their "best" position. Because they lived in fear of losing their best status, they destroyed opposition. They were something because they forced others to be nothing by comparison.

Daily in the classrooms of Knoe the children would remember St.. Michael for the dignity he gave to all mankind.

Thank you St Michael, for having lived,
For guiding us like a true parent
For encouraging choice,
For giving the world freedom and peace,
For allowing us to grow tall and wise..
...HAIL TO THE SECOND BEST.

THE SLOPING GARDEN

It was convenient and appropriate to the times that the Garden of Memories Cemetery had a terrain which sloped. Where a body was laid to rest on that incline was based on a judgment. Since God's judgment had to do with the goodness or badness of a person, certain men of the town felt it entirely appropriate, and not infringing on the rights of God, if they laid a person according to his "BEST' status.

In life the best were clearly at the top of the heap. These were the competitive mongers who would get to the top at any cost at the expense of pain and deprivation inflicted on others. They left in their wake casualties and never looked back. Never would they reach down, in the spirit of St. Michael, and lift another up and say, ""GO, be better than mc." The bodies upon which empires were built never received plaudit, yet without those sacrifices, the empires would not have been erected. It was not without justification that, at the entrance of the Garden of Memories there was a reminder to all who entered that sacred plot, a sign. HAIL TO THE SECOND BEST.

The arrangement was made: Those in life who practiced being at the top, namely the best, earned the bottom of the hill status. Those in life who practiced being at the bottom, yet pushing others upwards, whether intentionally or unintentionally, earned the top of the hill position.

Zeph was not pleased, nor was he displeased, to hear of his mother's demise. It was mainly another opportunity to ask someone for the return of his property.

Ariffa was more entrenched in the concern for Tillie's two children. It did her ego no good to be slighted the way she had been and, like an elephant, she would not forget. Being herself, she could not forgive.

Charlesmagne could not be reached and Ariffa's brother in Cincinnati was tied up with his own business and could not come.

Isidore rated Tillie for the top of the Garden of Memories Plot. Ariffa thought it was near the bottom.

Tillie never gave her children a dad; her principles would not allow it. She was interested in her own rights and neglected her children. If she were second best, her children would have become a source of pride, the best. As it were, they had become even less than she. a violation of nature's rule. She did not leave her lot in life better upon leaving this life, but worse. She left a retard and an arm-cutter behind.

Isidore objected. "She left me behind." She loved me; she needed me. She under-girded me when 1 was down and soothed my wrinkled brow. She was a mother to me, a genuine second best because she made me feel like "THE VERY BEST."

"But why not her own?" a voice challenged.

"Isidore spoke, "They were young. She had no gift with the young. If she had a beginning when they were older...perhaps."

With the evidence in, the decision was made. Mr. Peterson, Administrator of the Wc-Care Home, who was selected by the Peace Committee in these matters, had assessed the evidence. Tillie would rest neither at the top or bottom, but in the middle.

THE MAKING OF NATURE TO TREMBLE

Father Abe was concerned about the many victims of the Bull who were scattered throughout the outlying districts. Families were being split in half, children and the mother on one side and the father on the other. Though the Bull did not originate the new revisions in family structuring, he gave a mighty impetus to the family called the one parent family.

Where did that stress go, the stress that existed between countries? Did it go into space, like heat waves? It merely floated down, like feathers from a big goose in the sky, and landed in places which knew a wonderful, ecstatic bliss, of professed, undying love. There, a scurrilous stranger intervened called HURTING.

If the hurting is taken and placed in a circle, each time the circle turns it tears at the hide of the once beloved. The argument was like that. With its birth a season of unhappiness would begin.

Earlier, in tranquil, loving limes, one could settle for second best. Now the struggle is against it. Each wishes to be first, right, and the best. Oh, when that awful argument would show, as sure as the moon is round, unhappiness would surely grow.

In consequence, when no best is relinquished and no second best chosen, there is no love. Where there is no love, nature weeps

From the argument's ashes rose that dreaded emotion, HATE, which made nature tremble. Now the devastation that once occurred between countries had settled down on a little house in a little town, anywhere.

There is no hatred so vicious as that which flows out of a love factory; but also, there is no love so lovely.

If only hate would stop its rampage, but it wishes a destructive ill. It wishes not only that the sparrow fall, but that it plummets. It wishes that another be the dregs of second best exercising no will. It wishes that one who was loved dearly once, be subtracted from existence.

"Drop dead" was the popular wish...and so powerful, it could last more than twenty years.

Even nature has its contingency plans. If you can neither strive to be best, nor second best then you have forfeited your existence. You live but you don't live.

Nature has spoken.

A DOUBT IN TEACHING HONESTY

Mayor Culp wished to have the children impeccably honest and urgently requested that class materials for the first grade honesty class be on his desk in the morning.

"Beware of honesty," Isidore cautioned him.

Mayor pondered Isi's warning. Then doubt crept in; then fear.

The next morning, Father received a call from the Mayor, who now had completely reversed his thinking in the matter.

"It can blow the lid off the town. Abe," said the Mayor apprehensively.

"But the parents want it, Seth. We can't find a single parent who opposes it."

"But what they want and what they're going to get is not the same, Abe," the Mayor shouted. "Do you guarantee that what you have written down as material for an Honesty Class will produce no heartaches, no strife...?"

"We've done it with the blessing of the School Board. Rachel Brink helped with the content. Dr. Stout approved, Dr. Proud had no objection and Arriffa Plover found it extremely necessary...but no, Seth. I have no guarantees."

Father Abe's position had the strength of a straw in a gushing waterfall compared with the Mayor's driving concern for his popularity and his political stature.

THE BIRTH OF HACKE CRAMM, THE BELLRINGER

Two young lovers lay in each other's arms. Not a single noise could be heard in that remote area of town except the slight squeaking of the bed and light dripping of a faucet.

They were embracing. Some indirect light from the bathroom gave them twilight enough to see their bodies. The man pulled apart gently. The man raised his head and looked down at the region of his thighs.

"Nothing." he murmured. His feelings were mixed.

Again he embraced his woman companion, this time more passionately.

"This is good enough," he rationalized, not nearly believing what he was saying.

There, in that bedroom, fifteen years ago, was born the bellringer in Hacke Cramm.

Since then he triumphed over silence with a bell noise, unable to settle for a little noise and a little silence. Because he could not be in-between, he felt tortured. He could not be good enough to be normal and, being hurt harshly he could, some day, hurt back.

For a full week, Father would be devoting his total self to Hacke. His first encounter at the hospital found Hacke sitting at the edge of his bed, pretending he was holding a huge object in his hands. He imagined a penis, a thoroughly capable, potent penis. He made it so huge because he intended to use it on many women.

Father could see immediately that Hacke was triumphing over his little penis. After all, his mother made it clear to him that his writing wasn't big enough to suit her.

She called him a "Blackberry" and everyone on his block knew a "blackberry" was ugly. When she got to his lips, she could only say. They are too blackberry-ish."

The rule not only came first in the Hacke Cramm home, it was paralyzingly first. Being a true victim of the Rampant "NO," all day he listened to: "Don't lie, don't steal, don't cheat, don't get angry, you Blackberry." Every sentence started with a "Don't." Consequently he knew only what not to do. In order to be balanced he also needed to hear what he should do.

Hacke always expected someone to be dissatisfied with him, Father learned, his collar unfastened, his ears and eyes alert and his mind was open to the fascinating revelations which he had volunteered to become heir to.

Father was innately sensitive to Hacke's need to feel good enough. Being taught he was different, he would strive excessively to feel important, like being Jesus Christ.

Hacke described a picture of an alligator he once saw. It was pulling a defenseless, young animal by the leg into a water hole to drown it. Father's attentiveness assimilated every ghastly detail in the eyes of the creature as it was about to be devoured.

That same terror and agony was depicted in the eyes of Hacke who cried, "That's my face." Like a leaden object falling from a great height Hacke's head dropped into Father's lap, consumed in anguish.

Slowly, Hacke raised his face and pointed, inviting Father to witness Jesus Christ suffering in the nearby Plaza.

Father looked. An excellent view of the Plaza was-possible, but there was no cross. There was no Jesus Christ.

Hacke's father was a brilliant Doctor with an I.Q. of 150, but, remembering his ego-dismantling force and his awesome rage was enough to make Hacke's bed quiver. If he knew what his son was playing with beneath the covers that would spell total destruction.

Hacke had no choice; he had to be good before he could be natural.

"That son-of-a bitch," swore Father, completely abandoning his usual manner, but being, nevertheless, intensely honest.

"Why did you say that?" Hacke asked, surprised at Father Abe's language. "Because he hurt you. "

He looked up at father, reached for a glass of water, drank, then set it down.

"I almost feel as if 1 don't mind deciding to let up on some goodness," he asserted, cautiously.

Father knew Hacke was forced by his parents to be good, to be moral out of intense fear of the immoral and because of the rules, rules, rules, Hacke was immobilized. Without having a hand in it he was destined to be an unproductive, useless, second best.

"But why?" he pleaded, squeezing Father's elbow.

"Because they did not love you," came the honest but hurtful reply.

With raised fists, with streaming tears and pleading eyes, Hacke asked bitterly, "Then why did they have me?"

"To destroy you, Hacke."

"But why?"

'They had to be the best, Hacke; they had to be the first," said Father, feeling exhausted. "You became the grist for enhancing their egos. They could be something only if they made you nothing."

Bitter wailing could be heard by the nurse, sitting behind a counter far down the hallway. She knew it was none other than he who would ask any female for intercourse, loosening up. Father knew Hacke was willing to be an immoral something rather than a moral nothing.

"Be what you wish," Father said, "But realize that being immoral is attempting to triumph over being moral. It's a defiance. You couldn't call your father a bastard for hurting you, but you could defy him and hurt him by being immoral."

Eventually Hacke could see his over-reaction. He called it "shooting over the horse."

Hacke was neither moral nor immoral. In Father's view, he was "just right."

"I'm satisfied with your handwriting," he told him. "1 am pleased with your tiny handwriting.-and your penis is just right. As a matter of fact, I would not change a single cell in your body."

"So, I've been overshooting the horse?" Hacke repeated.

"If you weren't treated like dirt, you wouldn't act as if you were a Messiah."

"Then Hitler, can 1 be a Hitler?"

"I'm glad you want to be a Hitler. I'm glad you also want to be Jesus, Hacke...

" But I'm still overshooting the horse."

"I'm happy for you," said Father with a profound thankfulness. "At least you are not sprawled out under the horse, doing nothing. You are rebelling because you have no choice, and you want a choice. You are saying, I want to be first for a change. I am Hitler; I am Jesus: notice me.'

Hacke nodded his head approvingly. His tear ducts had dried up substantially.

THE WAYS OF DR. DANIEL PROUD, FATHER

Nothing was bad; nothing was wrong.

Can you raise five sons and a daughter without saying, "that's wrong?"

In the Proud home there was no wrong. There were errors, things were forgotten, there were mistakes, there was goofing off, there was swearing, there was ripping-off, there was playing one against the other, there was speaking out what's on your mind, there was lousy judgment, there was doing what you want to do providing it did not cause a riot or violate the law, there was free thinking; there was defiance and anger, but there was no wrong.

There was no wrong because what a child did was partially right To be called a four letter swear word isn't all wrong, not if you can notice in the voice a higher pitch and quality suitable for singing lessons,

"....and I'll pay for them," Dad Proud offered.

Any child who does his best deserves an extra amount of freedom. How wonderful to sign Dad's name to an excuse and succeed in fooling the principal. It's not all wrong; it's resourceful. It requires independent thought...but if you abuse the freedom you are no longer resourceful. You arc foolish.

Finally the pink slip comes. "You must punish Pude because he skipped class."

Not in the Proud family, not if Pude is doing his job. Not when his grades are all "A's." In fact Dad Proud recommends to the Principal, as an incentive for all students, a skipping-a-school day of their choice if they earn all "A's."

Reasonable defiance is welcome in the Proud family. It signifies that a child wants to grow up, to be a man. It is not wrong in the presence of good judgment; it may even be essential to cope successfully in life.

The guiding Principle in the Proud home is "Don't hurt yourself...wait, look at your alternatives, then, with good judgment, choose."

There is also a moral guideline: "It doesn't matter how smart you are if you are not also GOOD."

CAN TEACHING HONESTY HAVE A BACKLASH?

The Mayor wasn't kidding. Within a week he was on the tube appealing to parents to rescind their initial support for honesty classes. He even called them "Wrong."

From that moment his influence began to wane.

"Honesty was right, never wrong," retorted the group mind.

Since he could not change a single mind, he withdrew his opposition completely, allowing the will of the people and the committee to take its course.

Then the Mayor had received a stinging rebuke from the people as well as a forceful backlash which was unanticipated. They demanded that he expand honesty teaching to include all of the school children.

THE BISHOP'S FEAR

Meanwhile, Father Abe was writing to his Bishop about the new developments.

Many months had passed since Father's encounter with Bishop Jewel at his residence. Though he communicated with him regularly in writing, he heard nothing in return.

It was from Brother George, who was assigned by the Bishop to help relieve the work load of Father Abe, that he heard of a rumor. Father's correspondence was being stacked away, unopened.

If true, Father Abe surmised, the Bishop is afraid of being contaminated by his reports. Could it be that he was unwilling to trust himself with the knowledge of their contents and decided there was greater safety in knowing less?

Father Abe held his sixteenth report in his hand.

It told of the significance of the family, the love factory, in which Father was privileged to see depicted, almost daily, the manifestations of selfishness.

He wrote at length about value in the family system.

"Nobody has value in the world," he wrote, "except what he means to someone else's self-interest."

He gave a discourse on selfishness, its omnipresence, its hurting features, its need to be exalted to a place of a virtue and how to neutralize the fear associated with it.

...And love... He contended that love should be perceived more broadly, as an obedience to the rule of nature. "If nature says to man, as it does to every living thing, "Grow, mature" and man, obedient to its wishes says, 'I will,' that is love."

It is a gift of God that the full bloom of man is not achieved only by the love called caring but also by the love called listening to the voice of nature and participating in its message.

Alter explaining the plan for honesty classes in the town, the sixteenth report to Bishop Jewel was finished.

"If only he would read this one," Father hoped. The Bishop would find that he was more obedient than wayward. Perhaps Bishop Jewel could even agree that the pathways chosen by both men were divergent but, further down the road, they had a coming together.

TILLIE'S EARRING

Queenie was scheduled to see the Gynecologist ,

She thought it would be fun to wear something that belonged to Tillie. She examined the jewelry which she had inherited, handling each piece carefully. There were gold pieces, silver, platinum and three diamond-studded brooches.

Queenie had missed her period and wanted to have it checked out finally deciding on wearing an earring shaped like a rabbit's foot for good luck.

The Doctor had completed his examination and obtained appropriate test results. He looked up at Mrs. Krasno and, for the first lime, saw her earring. There was only one, not two. The initial curiosity prompted a closer look at the dangling entity.

Queenie removed the earring and handed it to the Doctor who wished to examine it more closely. He touched it; he smelled it. He took scrapings from it and studied them under a microscope. He had seen the likes of it before.

Queenie's solitary earring was a fetus.

At last. Queenie found Tillie's third child, dangling from her ear.

"It could have been me," said Isidore on receiving the shocking news from Queenie.

Isidore couldn't look inside the small box with a white rose on top which his wife prepared tenderly for a burial.

"Throw it away," some members of the group mind shouted.

Isidore couldn't He saw himself in that third, beginning child. It was the child he replaced in Grandma Tillie's life. He could not throw it away any more than he could throw himself away.

Isidore realized that Tillie had always supported free choice. A woman could choose whatever she wished to do with her body and she practiced what she preached.

With his frequent trips Isidore knew the nooks and crannies of the town of Knoe as well as any veteran cabby. There was a section of that town which probably never heard of Tillie Plover. They certainly were not heeding her advice, with four, six or more children to a family.

To Tillie free choice was basic. Abortion was a right.

The minority group which existed on the borderline level of poverty was neither interested in free choice, nor abortion. They were interested in having children. Children represented wealth. Since they could not be rich with money they would be rich with children.

With sadness. Isidore could see a reckoning. Tillie was putting her children on earrings; the poor minorities were giving their children life. Tillie's practice wasself-destructing. One hundred years from now, what was her family prognosis? What would be left of her offspring, Charlesmagne and Zeph Plover and one earring?

One hundred years from now what would happen to the poor family with six children. By then they would have multiplied many times over and extended their presence to well over 300 human beings. "These will inherit the earth," concluded Isidore.

Isidore decided to bury the small box with the rose in the Garden of Memories Cemetery. Mr. Peterson, who continued to be in charge of these matters agreed that an unborn was always designated as second best, mostly because they never had the opportunity to become best. The fetus would be placed at the highest level, above its mother.

The day was lovely. The residents of the WE CARE Home looked up. Across the street, at the top of the nearby hill, a crowd of not less than one hundred stood, all heads bowed. Father Abe looked down at a tiny match box\ carefully placed in the middle of a 6 foot by 3 foot excavation. He removed a vial of holy water from his pocket and sprinkled it on the box. Everyone knelt as he blessed the tiny container. Then, addressing the contents of the tiny container, he prayed:

"I give to you the heart of God,
A soothing, healing light.
Outstretched arms, the Lord is there.
Consoling Day and Night.
The "O" in God is Bosom,
To hug you when you cry,
A chamber in His precious heart
Where all the weary lie."

Isidore sighed deeply, his face blushed with emotion....but there was one thing missing....a name.

Isidore whispered to the Priest.

"May the soul of Isidore Plover forever rest in peace," he prayed.

THE NIGHTMARE

It was morning. Isidore was just relating a frightful dream to Queenie.

"It was a nightmare, Queenie; look at me shaking. Quick, pour me some coffee."

"How did you say you woke up this morning, precious?"

"Had my right toe in my left ear."

"Odd! Didn't know you could do that Isi."

"Had no choice. It was a matter of life or death. I was sleeping good then, all at once. I saw Death talking to a small kid. He wasn't born yet."

"Brrrr...scary."

"Death says to the cherub: "You'll only take your first breath on the condition that ya ain't aborted first. The only reason you're goin' to live is if a million conditions are right...but you'll be back," he said," in a hundred years or so, on the condition you don't come back in the first ninety-nine."

"Death hated to see the little fellow go." 'Life is a stream of conditions.' he warned 'em. 'You're goin' out there on the condition your heart is beatin' and no killin' germs are gettin' into ya. I tell you kid," he kept warning him, "It's dog-cat-dog out there. You got to fight to survive. Soon as ya get out the condition - baggers, cousins to the carpet baggers. Willl be waitin' for ya by your crib and everyone will spell out a condition or twenty for your livin.' They'll say, if you're gonna keep breathin.' their condition elixir will keep ya breathin' longest. And if ya don't go their way they'll call ya crummy, bad. stupid, spoiled rotten, possessed and a cockeyed runt."

" 'Do yourself a favor, kid. stay dead,' Death was saying. 'Ya got it peaceful here and no conditions. They got conditions and no peace; 1 got no conditions and peace.'"

"Then the baby speaks up, squeeky voice and all: "But I'll be breathin, 'feelin' the warm sun; I'll be eatin' fancy foods, screwin' around, goin' to college'..."

"Ya won't be breathin' if you're born on the moon or in Los Angeles." replied Death; 'you'll enjoy the sun only if it don't burn ya; you'll be eatin' fancy foods on the condition you ain't born in India; you'll be screwin' on the condition some girl's dad don't blow your head off first; and you'll go to college if you're smart enough and don't end up in a coal mine or prison. You might even live in a nice house providin' you ain't born a Zulu or an Kskimo.

After all that, if you're still livin'. baby, it's "cause you got the right medicine and a herd of giraffes didn't trample the guts out of ya, no water rose above your head, and no plane crashed with you aboard. Man,' Death was saying, 'You're really goin' to run a maze out there!

Oh, Oh...you're movin'...so I see you're ready to go anyway. Well, get ready to run the maze. I'm gonna be right behind ya.

"Where ya goin'. Death?" the kid asked..

"'Didn't ya know, kid? we go out together. I stay with ya waitin' for them conditions to get so rough on ya you can't tell your butt from a loaf of bread.. .Everybody out there will be doin' the same, protectin' their survivin'. Nobody out there is goin' to say, 'I'd rather die instead of you'...nobody."

Then the infant tasted something. "It's awful salty in here all of a sudden."

"Looks like ya ain't goin' nowhere, kid. They figure you're goin' to spoil their fun so they're comin' after ya. I hope they don't chew you up into hamburger meat for the dogs.

But don't let it get to ya. kid. All they see is what inconveniences you cause if you live, not what good they gain from your livin'.

"Stay here," Death beckoned. "You'll see 'em all come by anyway, but maybe a little sooner now, 'cause they don't know how much they're hurtin' themselves. Ya really love 'em kid, givin' up your life so they can enjoy their livin'. They'd never do the same for ya-"

"Hold my hand, Queenie." Isidore asked.

"But you're trembling, precious?"

Isidore continued.... "After two hundred years the abortionists ran out of conditions for survival; the over-sixty-five got knocked in the head next; then the gray heads and the bald heads lost their rights. Then the anti-abortionists got rid of the abortionists.

"But precious, how come you woke with your right toe in your left car?" asked Big Queenie.

"Running out of conditions, they finally came up with one that scared the shit out of mc. They said, "you breath if ya shove your right toe in your left ear.'

"You'd think that was impossible, wouldn't you? But if you've got to live, baby, you'll do it. Get the liniment, Queenie."

THE CONTINUING CHALLENGE OF HACKE CRAMM

As a giving person Father Abe rarely knew what he gave, unless it was concrete and down to earth. He could give an apple; he could give a stone and he could know the difference between both. But when he gave someone caring, he could not hold it in his hand, but he felt it. Subjectively, he might say, "It felt just right."

Father followed in the footsteps of St. Michael who gave value and importance to everyone. His intent was to remove obstacles which interfered with the river's smooth flow.

St. Michael's most remarkable quality, one that Father practiced to perfection, was the willingness to listen and obey.

Everyone wanted to lead, but to give value and importance, that required being a servant to the one in need. If a caring person obeys, he respects the expectations of both nature and of God.   Then he has both on his side. Such was the wisdom of St. Michael.

The group mind would ask, "What is his plan?"

He must have had some American Indian in him because he followed the twisting of the stream. He would turn here or swerve there, allow this, and elude that. Whatever came up he allowed value and importance to triumph.

Father Abe wanted to emulate the giving character of St. Michael in caring for Hacke Cramm. For weeks and weeks he had faithfully come to the Bellringer's side. Now he was coming with whole wheat bread and tea. It was something Hacke saw on a neighbor's table when he was three.

They gave him some, but he always wanted more.

He could even endure the beatings of the children who lived in the neighborhood who stood in his path, for a possible handout of whole-wheat bread and tea.

At home it was sour milk and eggs, which he hated. Nobody heeded his preferences for food at home, nobody listened; nobody cared.

Father prepared the tea, placed a hunk of bread in a dish and carried it to Hacke.

The aroma of the tea along with the flavor of the wheat bread made Hackc act child-like. He was a boy again, finding a new toy. For a while he did nothing else but eat. drink and sniff.

Hacke was being allowed his need. The whole world had its need also It was the same to Father, one person or a whole world; the need was universal. ...and peace was the derivative of the need fulfilled. Father believed it because it was then, in front of his eyes.

"More?" Father asked, willing to use the whole stockpile of bread and tea, if necessary, to satiate Hacke.

Hacke was full. Slowly he removed the covers, sat up on the edge of the bed and slid his feet into two slippers. Then he walked toward Father.

"I must do this." he said, bending over and pressing his meaty lips against father's cheek.

Hacke was learning to trust Father Abe. His word was reliable. There would be fresh whole-wheat bread and tea on the menu again. He was so confident in receiving it that he had fifteen lumps of sugar ready to add to the feasting.

Father was delighted to hear that he used connivance to acquire the sugar. At least he went after it and did not feel unworthy.

Whichever way Hacke went to achieve a release from his bondage, that was the way Father liked it.

Then came another weekend, a long weekend.

"But what will 1 do?" Hacke asked, his eyes searching frantically about the room.

He wanted to experience that protectiveness, that caring, forever.

"What is the penalty for murder, Father?"

"I know you are capable of killing. You have held your feelings down for so long that they can only shoot out explosively," said Father calmly, careful not to appear frightened.

Hacke could see how he overshot the horse again with his impulse to strike back. He knew what he was doing, but it did not always stop him from doing it.

Father would not leave Hacke empty-handed. He deposited a substantial remainder of the whole wheat bread and tea bags on the tray next to Hacke's bed and shook his hand reassuringly.

"I will be here Tuesday, at 8 a.m."

Hacke would depend on Father Abe's word, it gave him comfort and strength.

Having made provisions for Hacke's survival over the long weekend. Father left the building for the first time in three days. He had been experiencing a new side of life, a mother holding a child close.

On Tuesday.morning at 8 a.m. Hacke Cramm was gone.

He left a written message telling Father that he was not Jesus Christ. Neither was he Hitler. He was good enough.

THE DUFFY WAY

A massive array of exploded firework fragments littered the ground. Mary Duffy had just used up her reserve of fireworks. She exploded them a bit carelessly, thinking she heard Hacke Cramm's tingling bell in the neighborhood.

Mary was rocking back and forth and moaning when Father Abe arrived. A physician was attending to her hums. Two policemen stood nearby, cognizant that the city's ordinance banning fireworks was violated on the premises of the Duffy Camporee.

Father surveyed the environment, then decided to walk to a distant shed. He was seeking the whereabouts of Foxy Harold.

Before he could reach his destination he was called back by the physician who was attending to Mary Duffy. He needed help because Mary was refusing to lie down.

For a half hour the Doctor tried his best to move her. He spoke kindly, then harshly.

Mary sat trance-like, unmoved, persisting with a rocking motion and emitting haunting sounds.

Physical intervention seemed to be the only recourse. With a wave of his arm, the physician beckoned to the two policemen.

'"Wait," Father Abe shouted, as he remembered how the uncooperative were managed on the Duffy Domain.

He turned to Mary but did not bend over consolingly. He stood erectly, like a sergeant preparing a drill, and commanded, "Go to bed. It's the Duffy Way."

The enfeebled creature promptly stopped her rocking and. with a brief moan, which cleared her lungs, she lifted herself up, limped into the house and went to bed.

Mary Duffy's loyally to the Duffy Way was an unyielding force within her. Nothing could surpass it except her loyalty to one man. Hacke Cramm, known as Ihe Impotent Bellringer. To her he was one in a million. No penalty was too great for her to pay to have the meaning of his existence sustain her.

Mary wanted to give Hacke a personal message. She had dismantled her fertility-bearing mechanism years back. She actually had her hysterectomy to match his impotence, wanting him to feel better about himself by inflicting a parallel deficiency in herself. She loved him lhat much.

"But where is Foxy Harold?" Father asked.

Mary turned her head away.

"Gone," she said," as of January 1st. He got tired of the shed, promising himself that he'd start a new life. Figured there were plenty of other quiet places he could hide." Mary sighed, holding up her burnt hand toward heaven.

There was more in that boy than meets the eye, Father. Guess you never know your own kin until they leave, he even patted me on the head. Never before did he touch me like that, never before."

Father told Mary that her 10 years of fireworks hoarding was over. Hacke was no longer a noise hound.

It meant he would be coming soon.

Mary rested. For hours she slept with a peacefulness that she had never known, sedated by the vision of two lovers reuniting.

THE ABSENCE OF EGOISM

Harvey Calsbeke had a great deal lo do with the creation of THE MUSEUM, WORLD WITHOUT EGOISM.

The Peace Group had, for some time, accepted the inevitability of selfishness. Not only did the committee sanction it but observed that it was rampant. It agreed that, when a person told another. "Don't be selfish," that person meant, "My type of selfishness is better than your type."

When Harvey examined his work in Value and Importance, he was positive that he was feeding egos. When Vivian heard his message on the radio it caused the swelling up of her ego. Compliments were good for the ego, success was good for the ego.

Harvey began to wonder if man really cared the for anything or anybody except himself. What a massive illusion, he thought, to be caring for someone else.

What did nature have in mind to make so many people and men make each one ego-oriented, a personal center of the universe, and then hid each to survive. It was a contest. It was like tossing him into a world crawling with ego-starved lions. And who would the winner be? The strongest, the fastest, the wittiest, the best in any category worthy of merit.

"Man primarily serves himself," Harvey concluded..But the serving of self was such a wise, wise move. If it was God who concocted the idea, then God was a genius. How else can a person survive unless he serves himself, outwitting other egos, abusing other egos and even defending other egos.

Harvey decided, when each person alive serves himself, he adds a commonness to his existence. In other words, he is doing what every one else is doing. Therefore. being predictable, it adds stability to man' existence. By serving himself man is better able to know himself and his neighbor. Man is not self-serving just to be self-serving; he is self-serving to be consistent with his fellow man, so there may be order in life.

What if man did not serve himself? Harvey asked. To depict this state of man, THE MUSEUM ON A WORLD WITHOUT EGOISM was created with the help of many volunteers.

Various wax-images are arranged in separate compartments as one enters the structure. In the first compartment there is an office setting. The boss reminds his assistant that he will be receiving a raise and promotion. In the next scene, the assistant pours coffee over his boss' bead.

Moving on, in an adjacent compartment, is a beautiful woman., 20 years of age, well educated, talented, socially admired with numerous suitors. In the next setting she is marrying a 92 year old man who is penniless. He can hardly walk. His main means of subsistence is what he can scrape from the neighborhood garbage cans. He has no teeth and he hasn't bathed in weeks.

In the next compartment, a man has just purchased a beautiful Cadillac. He has saved up all his life for that moment. He takes a crowbar and starts to dismantle it, piece by piece, until it becomes a heap of junk. Then he will hose it down with water and lime and watch it rust away.

THE MUSEUM ON A WORLD WITHOUT EGOISM has made its point. Take away the self-serving aspect which permeates the whole human species and what have you? Indescribable irrationality and chaos and complete abandonment of good judgment.

THE BEST LEAVE HURTING IN THEIR WAKE

Thank God for Harvey Calsbeke, the second best, who is a life preserver, seeing to it that others survive well. With Value and Importance he would attempt lo increase their esteem and they could then feel more worthy to be self-serving. What is he, but an ally of nature, assisting it in its quest that man may survive even better.

Harvey liked to encourage the selfish side of man to become best.

Some became best for now, living with the illusion that you live forever. These trampled on others and left in their wake a sea of hurting in order to reach the top at any cost. For them the end was a tragedy. They lived on the premise that they were indestructible and money would fix everything.

Others became second best to those who would blossom as best in the future. They would have nurtured their best talents, practiced the best in growing-up techniques, feeling satisfied that they responded to the expectations of a family life.

HAIL TO THE SECOND BEST

Orkway, that citadel of baser urges, protector and keeper of society's misfits, loomed not far in the distance. Not more than a gray mirage, its mystique could hardly be known from the vantage point of a cattle drive. The drive was a replay of the olden days having the sound and sober reason for being, to cut costs for the film makers.

The heifers came through over the south ridge from the ranch lands to the West, horses protectively at their side, steered them away from the shelter belts which beckoned to them for refuge. The riders' puffed clothing fattened men as they skillfully swerved the strays to a right direction. A wagon of straw in front but a snowball's throw from their steaming noses enticed them. From the back they were prodded, at their sides guarded, and in front they were baited.

But Doc was too involved in negotiations at the local sports arena to witness the site.

I saw that the students were not in the mood for compromise, not if they claimed the title, "WINNERS." They wanted to be number one decisively, even if by one second or one point. They wanted all honor and ignored Doc Proud who reasoned with them, that the winners needed losers to win, and they too should have recognition.

"It was insulting. You don't ponder on losers; you forget them. They arc nothing but past history, the routed vermin from the farmer's orchard," contended the students.

Parents agreed, but it should be done quietly, to avoid a riot

A letter was acceptable, but it should not be duplicated that it might fall in the wrong hands. It was also reasonable if the coach told the losers that they did a good job.

The Athletic Association refused to have the loser on the same level as the winner. The advice for the loser was clear: they should work harder.

Finally, Doc suggested a mere moment of silence for the loser.

"Everyone would be jumping around and hugging each other." he heard. "The bedlam wouldn't permit it. The winner would be too excited and, furthermore, you can't possibly have a jubilant crowd going out the door and suddenly stop for a lousy silence."

Doc had an idea..."Let's do it in the middle, at intermission time. That way we won't know the winner, we won't know the loser either…"

That was the greatest insult of all. He would be recognizing nobody at all because, when the game is over, both teams plan to be winners.

Doc Proud was challenged by the group mind.

For several days he researched the tactics of the world famous diplomats, Gromyko, Dulles, Acheson, Kissenger. Then he studied the great educators and theories on discipline. He was willing to do anything to infringe on the hackneyed ritual where winners take all and losers are cast into a cheap basket.

Then he had a brainstorm, the Ditties.

Ordinarily that sweet-singing group would barge in anywhere and begin chirping right into your bean soup, but not this time.

It took Doc a whole minute to diagnose the problem.

He called Guard Supervisor, Hal, at Orkway. Then he called Ariffa.

Because Cell 20, The Tomb, would now have a potty, the 40 Ditties consented to appear at the next game. They would wear Halloween costumes in February for contrast. They would sit together in one bunch during the whole game and, for both notice and voice practice, they would sing out the score each time a basket was made.

Finally, the game was over. By a deafening applause a winner emerged.

As anticipated, the exiting was rapid. Only the losers lagged behind. Their urgency to move had been reduced to a weak shuffle and their brains turned them into numbed robots. Some..downtrodden, cried and held their heads. Finally, they draggedthemselves, like a truckload of partially tranquilized cheetas to the showers to wash the muck and the shame from their Apollo-like bodies.

Then, from behind one group of lockers appeared a whole flock of Ditties with a "Ta,Ta"

From another appeared the winners yelling repetitiously, "We are number one."

Again a melodious, "Ta, ta" was heard. In the language of music which every decent human being respected. It meant, "WE ARE HERE; BE QUIET."

With the winners there, each holding up a finger, as if testing the wind direction and the losers here, shamefully looking at the cracks in the floor, the Knoc Town Ditties sang:

You are fast and we are last;

You are tall and we are small:

You have made the world so bright.

Everything you did was right;

Hail, hail, hail to the Second Best
Who make the Best prevail.
East and North and South and West
We've been good, but you are Best.
What we give, we give free
For now and all eternity...
Hail, hail, hail to the Second Best
Who make the World Go Round.
The number one finger was gone and the bowed heads were lifted.

Of course, it was common knowledge that a team forced to be second best could conceivably not like it. Team members might be enraged, friends of the team members might be angry and they might want to kick something.

"The kicking the dog syndrome" was an act of revenge against an innocent person or his property. In the nomenclature of the police, it was called, vandalism.

On the night of the game, especially if the Chicken Heads lost, the incidence of vandalism grew: Hedges pulled up by the roots, B-B holes in windshields, empty beer cans in corner mail boxes, eggs flung out of speeding cars, and tires suddenly leaking.

When the Ellendale Pot Bellies won, they were also dissatisfied. They wanted not only to win but to triumph, to "rub it in your face;" not only to win, but to go wild and break a window.

The Knoe Town Chicken Heads lost and were subdued. Instead of "Kicking the dog" they found another, more peaceful and redeeming outlet. They conceded, by actually congratulating the Potbellies, shaking hands, and even buying them cokes. Being satisfied, the Potbellies were defused and most satisfied with the win. There was no reason to do "nose rubbing."

"Hail to the Second Best" had become a popular cheer after games. It would de-triumph the winners, redeem the losers and reduce the incidence of vandalism, the Police reported, by 80%.

SELF-DESTRUCTING THROUGH TRIUMPHING

Last fall, the Musk-Oxen fullback was bashed unmercilessly and carried off the field. Father, protector of souls, stood sentinel over the beaten player.

Not even a hospital bed gave him fear; not the preparation for surgery, not the last rites.

"The Musk Oxen won." That was the totality of the moment..

"We beat the hell out of the Wolves. Father."

"And they beat the hell out of you."

The player flinched.

"It's nothing "

"When they called mc, you were unconscious."

"It's nothing."

"You were flattened by a ton of Wolves."

"Hazards of the game. Father, couldn't be helped."

"You could have handed them the ball?"

Father sounded remarkably stupid to the giant of a man.

"You don't win games that way." he said, a shining example of a true sportsman.

Father Abe was mostly concerned about the Fullback's survival. But the player was concerned with winning.

Father realized that he had met a person that he had only read about in sports magazines, a man to whom winning meant more than life itself, one whose triumphing was self-destructive.

Triumphing was ubiquitous. Stores had their subterfuges, disguised plain clothesmen, electronic devices, mirrors and cameras, all arranged strategically to enhance the final triumph, the decisive seizure of the shop lifter.

The law would triumph over the criminal, justice over injustice, the white hats over the black, good over evil, whites over black, Irish Protestants over Irish Catholics. Democracy over Communism, God over the Devil. Wherever there was winning there was triumphing.

"While many were triumphing, others were saying. "I haven't triumphed enough. By hook or by crook, 1 will triumph in trumps."

What was life anyhow, but a striving to triumph over your neighbor. To look at another and say. "I am better than you." I will survive ahead of you and in spite of you.

Into this climate of dog-eat-dog survival, the town of Knoe added a stratagem of hope and decency as a counterbalance. The concept, HAIL-TO-THE-SECOND BEST.

THE TEACHING OF RACHEL BRINK

"Once upon a time." Rachel Brink read lo her children from her Honesty Text. "There was a boy. His name was Doy."

"Doy, Doy," he said, when he greeted someone.

"Doy, Doy," others replied.

He loved his name very much.

Doy often went to the mountains to shout, "Doy, Doy," just to hear his echo shout back, "Doy, Doy."

In the logging camps in the mountains the men had a word which they used very carefully. The name was "Doy" also.

When a tall, heavy tree was about to fall, they yelled the word. It meant, "be careful, be alert, watch out"

It was a dangerous thing to do, to ""Doy" around the logging camps, but the boy just couldn't stop. He liked his name too much.

"The Doy was a habit" Rachel explained. "Habits had a character of their own. They were unable to appreciate the hurt they could cause. The Doy is very near, as close as a person's nose," she said. "That makes it very hard to see."

Rachel looked down at the fresh, eager faces in her First Honesty Class. She asked them to make a Doy out of the ordinary things they did daily.

A "Good morning" was suggested. That was to cheer somebody up. It was a friendly greeting.

"But can someone be hurt by a "Good morning?" Rachel asked them.

Mrs. Brink was challenging the well-rooted processes of her students' thinking. They were obviously taught one way, the nice way. To honestly look at how hurting might occur was clearly difficult for them because they were not accustomed to living that approach.

Finally, with some guiding and prodding from their teacher the students found it possible that a grouchy person might be hurt by a "good morning." Somebody Doying with a "good morning" for everybody might "good morning" a grouchy man and make him feel even grouchier.

Rachel certainly could not blame the children for what they were taught, which was to do the right thing. But she wanted to take them a step further, to have them see, in the drama of real life, how the right thing, though unintended, could have the wrong consequences.

Rachel reviewed the formula for improvement. "Be as you are," she read, "only see how friendly actions can hurt others." The students liked hearing it because they didn't have to change anything. They were believing that they were good enough. Thinking with the mind of a Second Best Rachel could easily understand that the most lasting, most welcome improvement came not from insisting on change, but allowing it to happen.

Next came the story' of a man who enjoyed fishing, but his wife did not. She became lonely. Eventually the family split in two., then they divorced.

The Doy was the fishing. The man cared more about his Doy. The couple were unhappy because the wife needed to be Best, instead she was treated as Second Best.

"Now we know what can happen if a Doy becomes more important than a person." Rachel pointed out.

Next came the example of the farmer and his wife. They had three children. The farmer had his farm and the wife tended to the children-

After the children were grown, the wife wasn't contented any more. Like the Fisherman's wife, she was all alone. He had his farm, but her children were gone.

The students identified the farmer's Doy. He was acting as if nothing had changed in that family. Suddenly, his farm came ahead of his wife. She became Second Best.

"What happens when we place something ahead of someone we love?" Rachel asked her group.

"They feel cheap."
"No good."
"Lonely."
"Sad."

It was the kind of Second Best the children never wanted to experience.

"Their first homework assignment was about Doys...to find as many as possible.

"When you sec a Doy hurting someone, don't be afraid of it," Rachel assured the children. That Doy was probably around a long time anyway. You'd just be noticing it"

The class left and Rachel was alone She looked about her classroom, her eyes fixated on a certain seat. She moved toward it. The name Tristan, was written at the corner of the desk.

Once upon a time Tristan Roe sat in that seat, Rachel recalled. He had a special contraption fastened under his desk for pedaling, a product of his father's resourcefulness.

Tristan was a phenomenon, born with very active legs which moved day and night.

In the months and years ahead the world would learn more about the foot pedaling youngster who, though he lived in a society where triumphing was rampant, had the uncanny ability to choose, either to be Best or Second Best.

Since his birth Tristan Roc was preparing himself for The International Star Foot Races in Helsinki. From his very first kick, he was off and running. Bed sheets had two convenient slits for his legs since he was always running, day and night.

Medical experts advised that Tristan was a sound, healthy baby who would outgrow his leg action when he started walking.

When it was time for Tristan to walk, he ran.

After four years of academic foot pedaling, his pedals began to squeak. His fine-grade oil, which he carried for such exigencies, proved ineffective. Consequently, Tristan was allowed 15 minutes, on the hour, to run around the school building. He ran everywhere he went. Not only did 'Frisian run, but he ran faster and further than other boys, some much older than he.

It never entered Rachel Brink's mind when Tristan sat in her classroom that he had those precious ingredients, a rare Chemistry, which had also accommodated the spirit of the town's beloved Saint Michael.

Day after day the school children discovered new Doys. Speaking became a Doy if it involved calling names; eating became a Doy when a brother cried because the older brother ate all of the cereal. Even walking could be a Doy if it meant stepping in a puddle of water with new shoes.

When the children realized how they could hurt others without meaning to, then they were in a better position to choose, to hurt or not to hurt. If they could avoid hurting others, then, for their consideration, they could be liked more, have more friends and even hurt themselves less.

Eventually, they had moved higher up and looked down. They could see more hurting about them. Within their own families they could see hurting. They could see it and were amazed that nobody was even speaking about it.

For days and weeks the children searched for Doys in themselves, but parents were growing impatient. They wanted Honesty, not Doys.

PROLIFERATION OF HONESTY

It was therefore, appropriate to move on to Chapter II of the Honesty Text entitled: WHAT YOU'VE ALWAYS WANTED TO SAY TO YOUR PARENTS BUT NEVER SAID BECAUSE YOU WERE AFRAID.

Rachel was aware that a family could have it's own group mind, where speaking out could be construed as offensive. Yet the children could see Doys in their parents. With silent prayers to St. Michael, Patron Saint of the Free Spirit in Man, the children were discovering a renewed courage to speak forthrightly.

To speak the truth was to speak honestly. It was exactly what the parents clamored for. What could possibly go wrong., thought Rachel.

It was time for Mayor Culp to become frantic. Parents would never allow anyone to dabble in their own honesty and that was his unshakable position. As leader and protector of the citizens of Knoe he would take precautionary measures.

With assistance of Dr. Stout's students, emergency squads were formed and stationed for immediate action. All wayward youth, ousted from their homes would be instructed to proceed directly to emergency shelters. There, stores of food, blankets and medical supplies would be available.

Finally, all was in readiness. The whole student body received their "HOW COME?" assignment simultaneously. It involved no reading, no writing but all home work.

"How come you make me feel as if I don't want to do what you tell me?

"How come you never say sweet words to each other?"

"How come, every time I go out you complain and how come you never say. 'Have fun.'"

"How come you don't care how I feel when you fight?"

"How come' you always tell me, "you don't mean that' when you must know I wouldn't say it if I didn't mean it?"

"How come you go to your bedroom when Father comes home from work?"

"How come you don't speak to each other?"

"How come you don't care how badly I feel when you treat me as if I can't do anything right?"

THE HURTING PLAGUE

Almost simultaneously, the "How comes" elicited the dreaded "BUT YOUS."

Unfortunately, the Mayor's prognostication was correct. A hurting plague was descending on Knoe Town.

The "But yous" rained down upon the children like darts of sleet, cutting through flesh-warm air. No amount of comprehension could obviate the brute force of a Goliath screaming, "Answer me; what do you mean by that crack?"

It was impossible for many children to escape castigation and punishments. But abandonment, that was a most painful price to pay for genuine honesty.

Those children who were fortunate enough not to be shaken physically were able to maintain lucid speech. Verbally, they were taught to reverse the process of dissension and would tell their parents, not the truth, but what they wanted to hear.

That soothed them, indeed, lulled them into a placid state of mediocrity. Their nice image was enhanced and they responded as the teachers had predicted.

The blaming petered out rapidly as' the children looked in astonishment. They were barely grown and were already practicing the commonest technique of the ages. The Embellishment of the Storefront

Unfortunately, not every child could effectively communicate the magical words before they heard the terse command..."GO."

No bone-crushing melee was more vicious as children walked meekly to the designated shelters.

Eventually parents emerged from their homes. Like guilt-ridden termites, they sought out their own. Reunions were often weepy, apologetic. At times emotions were confused; other times there were no feelings.

One small boy was unclaimed for several days. When Rachel brought him home she was astonished to hear the father say, "I'll take him back only if he tells me I'm right"

Rachel could feel the boy shudder as he clutched her hand.

"I don't think it's in him," Rachel said quietly.

The father wasn't convinced. "Am I right, boy?" he asked.

"He can't tell you you're right because he hasn't been given that same consideration. How can he tell you if he hasn't been told himself?" Rachel pleaded.

"Take him back," the father ordered.

Rachel was able to jam her shoe against the door in time to keep it from slamming shut.

Quickly, she proposed a compromise. Could she speak for the boy?

The father rubbed his chin, weighing the merits of Rachel's proposition.

He agreed"

Rachel hesitated. She cleared her throat twice.

Imitating a slurring idiot, she said, finally, "Yrnrr roght."

Finally, the "love" word was about to come forth, that indisputably decent word: "C'mon in son, I wouldn't take you back if I didn't make a commitment to love you."

"Commitment" was a word Rachel began to dislike. To her one was devoted and felt a natural, everlasting love with closeness and sharing, a feeling which would propel people toward bliss and happiness for years and years. Commitment was a product of the legal mind, not the loving heart.

In spite of the Hurting Plague which disrupted the routine of many families. Father Abe was pleased to find some households which remained astonishingly unperturbed. Children could tell their folks anything and they weren't about to be murdered. What kind of love factory was it that failed the screaming test when the whole neighborhood was sounding off? Was it the kind of home where the Best were being nurtured?

The likes of St. Michael and Tristan Roe came from somewhere... Father wondered.

Doc Proud was indeed pleased when he received a yellow ribbon for his mail box. That was the symbol which meant his brick domain remained tranquil.

Should father come nosing around, checking out the homes tagged with a yellow ribbon. Doc was ready. He had his narrative already typed for him: "Avoid restriction," it read. "If you are to err, err in favor of freedom. Give room forexpression. Don't bind a child's wings that wish to fly. Let his thoughts come forth and be a beacon for further learning. Let him read what he wants; let him see what he wants. How else will his judgment develop. How else will he choose correctly except that he is unbiased in his alternatives. Have faith that he will overcome, not fear that he will be devoured by a four letter word. He who chooses freely does not hurt himself. Who hurts himself is he who is not allowed to reasonably defy. He carries his rebellion to the street where the rampant NO turned into a defiant YES.

Woe to the destiny of offspring of parents who needed to be respected at all cost. They needed to be first but the children needed them to be Second Best. Meanwhile, an abused nature weeps."

Father Abe was distressed to learn that most children were ostracized, punished, screamed at, or shaken. The trauma had taken its toll. Corrections were required coming from squads of counselors trained to remove the hurt.

Rachel, anticipating a deluge of protests from irate parents, decided to get away with her children and discuss their reactions. Sitting in a field, on the grass, the children said,

"It was scary."

"It was the end of the world."

"It gave me hiccups."

"It made me want to run away."

After some group discussion, the children felt better.

Then they went to the Pet Cemetery at the edge of town. They browsed around, reading the cat, dog, fish and parakeet markers.

The students learned that animals meant a lot to some people. They meant so much that, even after the animal was gone, owners wanted to continue a relationship with the pet.

The children learned that the search to be a somebody to someone was going on everywhere. This gave Rachel an opportunity to open the door to the next class assignment: MEAN SOMETHING TO SOMEBODY.

CONFRONTING THE HURTING PLAGUE

Eventually, the town reverted to its usual calm which demanded that Father become busier, previously he would casually visit families and receive wonderful amenities and some drink, usually tea. His best guess, that a Pandora's Box of guilt was unleashed in the love factories, caused him no special distress. In fact he was grateful lo God for shaking the townsfolk. Their sedateness, their smugness required it entirely as much as a tree might require some wind to shake a defunct leaf

It was incredible to see the gauging currents of agony inflicted by nothing less than the truth.

It was two o'clock, the doorbell was ringing for the tenth lime. The tenth visitor was a member of a protest group, a father demanding that parents not be used for homework.

"Tell me what to do," he pleaded. "I realize my boy is absolutely correct. I do ignore him. I do take my wife for granted...but I was always like that."

The Father sat down on a sofa.

"How do I change?" he asked Father anxiously. "What must I do to improve? How can I do better?"

"What's to change?" Father responded flippantly. "You were always like that. There is only one difference, now you know it. Your son told you."

"But what Can I do? Do nothing."

The father was not content to be doing nothing. It wasn't productive. He wanted advice.

The opportune moment had come. The time was ripe for choice. Father would give him two courses of action to pick from. Before the Hurting Plague the father could only be one way, the hurting way. The Plague gave him an insight, another route.

"Hurt your family if you wish," Father proposed, OR ELSE STOP IT."

DANIEL AND CORA, JUST RIDING AND TALKING

Daniel and Cora Proud were driving home from Littlefield. If the Mayor of Littlefield was elected Governor, though his chances were looking excellent, Doc Proud had no intention of voting for him.

Mother Proud had a contrary point of view. New industries were being negotiated and the Mayor was influential in those matters. In fact, Knoe Town was being considered for the self-contained, plastic submarine plant to be constructed by the Japanese.

"But Orkway will go."

"You don't know that for sure, Hon? The Zephyr, his nephew, is still confined there. The lawyer told him that he was receiving $80,000 from his mother's estate and what does he do? He thinks his arm is a pork chop and he tries to cut himself to death."

"It's ghastly."

"..All because I refused to return his property."

"You kept something that belonged to him?"

"Razor blades."

Doc sighed as his wife held on to his arm.

"I may be out of work," he whispered.

I'll be here. Daddy."

"You mean you will be my cushion if I fall?"

"I'll be your cushion; I'll be your net; I'll be your cottonball."

Doc Daniel Proud felt good...in the face of adversity he fell a warm, secure comfort. God, he was happy to have someone on this earth doing that for him.

Then he heard a voice whisper as he drove along a straight road, "I love you very, very much, the man I chose for me. You have shared a rare, rare love called responsibility."

Doc felt needed and he felt loved. At that moment he was prepared to cope with any adversity. He didn't need five, not a hundred, not a thousand. He needed only one, one person....her.

An intense coziness and a great calm appeared to have been created within the interior of the 15 year gas-guzzling Cadillac as they cruised route 90.

Then Mother Proud asked Daddy Proud, "How come I call you Daddy and you call me Mother?"

"Don't know exactly, Mother...excect it has to do with meshing. We call each other what the children call us, Darling--it's part of family unity."

Some raindrops splashed on the wide windshield. Doc pushed a button.

"If those wipers were talking to you, what would that squeaking be telling you. Mother dear?"

"Scratch, scratch, scratch."

"To me it sounds like, was it right? was it right? was it right?"

" I love you."

"What did you say?"

"1 love you, 1 love you, I love you, I love you, it says."

"You're right, you're exactly right.

TRISTAN ROE WAS COMING HOME

Tristan roe was coming home. To celebrate the occasion, confetti nulls were pressed into action, school bands were alerted and decorators festooned the plane terminal with flower petals. A platform was being constructed for a choir of guitar strumming girls who would sing the Star Spangled Banner.

Tristan Roe and his performance in the International Star games highlighted the discussions of the townsfolk. Especially in the advanced honesty classes was the subject discussed intensely.

"If he won. we'd greet him with an ovation,." they postulated. "If he lost, the greeting would be appropriately mediocre."

"But what if he thinks he won?"

"That is a private victory. Then he claps tor himself."

Under Agreement and Helping, Principle 8. it reads. 'When you agree with someone, you pull together; when you disagree, you let him do it himself."

Picture this: Tristan emerges from the plane and he is the only one clapping."

"Consider this image: He emerges, raises his arms in victory and shouts. I won. I won,' but the crowd shouts hack. "You lost, you lost."

"That embraces the principle called The Immovable Object: 'If two agents want to be right, and they are contradictory, one must give in to the other to achieve stability. Otherwise there is dissension and debate.

"This awkward situation could have been avoided, if he had only won," observed a student.

"Events often do not proceed according to our wishes or convenience," responded another.

A book was reopened.

"Here it is, 'Dishonesty and Inconvenience, Postulate II'. Anyone who wants his own way is already reacting to an inconvenience."

"If you say you love someone but, instead, you defeat them , your popularity will suffer because you are not nice. If the rule says, defeat someone, but you love them instead, then you should be more popular because you portray the image of niceness."

"But even your niceness doesn't serve you if you produce an inconvenience which is traumatic enough."

Even in the college dormitories the discussions continued:

"What if he lost simply to lose. Would that be less popular than to lose so that another might win?"

"Your reference to losing to lose is purely hypothetical and irrational."

"I would want him to win big and wouldn't care shit for less."

"Page 72, Postulate 14, under Honesty and Frustration." Check it for yourself. 'If an individual does not live up to our expectations then we are disappointed, frustrated and angry."

TRISTAN MEETS DOROTHY

When he wasn't breaking into a jog in the aisles, Tristan was sitting with his new-found acquaintance.

Headed for Antioch, Dorothy said she was a student in Business Education.

Tristan assessed her as very ordinary, not particularly desperate-looking or deficient in any important aspect. She was certainly self-sufficient, the independent type.

Maybe Tristan wanted to elicit the feminine, more helpless qualities, in Dorothy. Perhaps he was beginning to feel competent enough and sufficiently generous in giving her his "Moment."

He would give her a moment for survival, an everything-for-you-and-nothing-for-me moment; a You-are-the-Best Moment; a moment fresh from the hearth of the love factory.

Even as he waited with Dorothy for the circular baggage conveyor to spin out with her luggage, he was already sensitive to the warmth in their relationship.

"That's it, that's the one."

The girl pointed to a pink back pack.

Dorothy hunched over.

"Put it on my back." she asked.

Tristan carried the heavy hulk himself. In a cab, they searched for the nicest eating place in town.

After their dinner together, Dorothy anxiously scanned the city environs just outside of her window, then excused herself

She returned, continually looking about.

"Anything I can do?" Tristan asked her.

She needed to make a phone call.

Tristan pulled out a pocket full of quarters.

"Here."

The change trickled into the cup of her hand.

The call was not fruitful. "He's not home." she said.

Tristan lugged the burdensome pack to a bus depot where Dorothy found a bus schedule.

Both sat on a concrete bench waiting for the bus from Edmunson Ave.

"What's the pack for?" Tristan asked.

"Traveling. Been to Mexico three times."

"Rich parents?"

"Lucky thumb."

"I don't want you to hurt yourself," said Tristan coarsely. "How will you return to Ohio?"

"Hitch hike."

"Take the bus instead," he said, with an obvious dash of displeasure. He reached into his pocket and squeezed a handful of dollars into Dorothy's hand.

The bus came, finally.

Dorothy stepped up, followed by the young man from Knoe, carrying an awkward-looking pink bundle. He stuffed it snugly against the ceiling of the bus.

He turned and received a "thank you" hug from Dorothy. Suddenly, flashbulbs popped and the interior of the bus brightened.

Tristan was airborne again alter reuniting with his team. His plane left just before the police had arrived to question him.

Someone had recognized Dolly Dirks on the bus with her arms around Tristan Roe, the controversial sports figure.

Dolly had an unglamorous history. She had evicted many old men and women from their cars and assumed possession of their vehicles. She was lucky, not because of her thumb, but because she accepted rides selectively, from someone she could easily cast out from a car with a single thrust of her leg.

Two pieces of information preceded Tristan to the town of Knoe. First was the clear insinuation that a businessman from Denver had made an arrangement with the Knoe runner to tamper with the Helsinki races. Second was the news that he had abetted the escape of Dolly Dirks, a vicious criminal.

TRISTAN CHOOSES "MOMENTS" TO LOSE

In the face of these events, Tristan landed on his home-town soil, anticipating no rancor or ill will, but a happy moment from the townsfolk.

Under the circumstances anybody present could know that, if ever there was a time, this was the time for the runner to have his big moment. Applause, recognition, heightened emotions...all for him, for that moment.

What he did or what they thought he did should be set aside. What counted was the person and his surviving because, if he survives, then they all survive.

Why are you here?" reporters asked the people who were intent on providing the desperately needed moment for Tristan.

"To applaud a loser."

"But why applaud a loser?"

"Because he is a winner among losers."

"And why are you here?" they asked others.

"Tristan refused to win. He is suspected of bribery and consorting with a criminal."

"Because he is a winner."

"But he didn't win."

"He said he is a winner."

'Yes, but he didn't win.""

"If he said he won, then he is a winner."

The people were speaking from the depths of the Love factory where logic is arbitrary, where events are secondary and survival is everything.

Tristan looked introspectively. Why had he chosen Everything-for-you- and nothing-for-me moments? Why did he let Cebu of Angola and Lebkowski of Poland win? He fell back because he singled them out and made them feel special and. later, when he heard, "Nobody has treated me like that in my whole life." he was thrilled. From then on. he knew be could never stop giving "MOMENTS."

But now he was hoping for a moment from the people.

A deafening cheer greeted Tristan as he stepped from his plane. A choir of guitar-strumming females sang the National Anthem, then another high-decibel cheer followed. When it subsided, Tristan spoke three words.

"What did he say," the people asked each other, just as the cord became detached somewhere, deadening the speakers.

The words spoken by Tristan filtered down so that those who stood in the rear eventually received the three-word message.

On hearing the words, the people decided to go home.

RACHEL TEACHES CHILDREN ABOUT LIFE

Three people stood in Rachel Brink's Honesty class. They were playing the "Yes-No" game.

"What is your name?" asked one girl.

"Joseph," replied the boy.

"It is not. It is Al" said the other girl.

"How old are you?" he was asked.

"Eleven"

"No, you're not, you're 8." the boy heard.

"What color are your eyes?"

"Brown."

"They are not. Your eyes are Blue."

The Yes-No Game went on and on.

Suddenly Joseph became dizzy. He chose dizziness to avoid experiencing any further contradictory message. Other students decided to act frozen, statues who refused to answer any more questions. Others decided to be mixed up. They were unsure, unable to tell what was true. Some were bothered by the game. With anger they protested and called the game "stupid."

Rachel asked if the children ever experienced any Yes-No messages elsewhere.

"On TV, the candy people say "yes, eat candy, but the Dentist says, no, don't eat candy."

"On TV the beer people say, 'Yes. drink it because it is light and less filling.' 'but the Doctor says,' No, don't drink it; it hurts your liver."

"The cigarette pack says, 'smoking is dangerous to your health.' Then what should a kid like me do when mom and dad smoke?"

More and more double messages were cited by the students of Rachel Brink's class. For the time being, knowing that opposite messages were part of their daily lives was sufficient. With that, they could better understand the inconsistencies in every-day living. They should not be afraid of the Yes-No situations but, instead, make up their own minds.

Rachel was teaching her students to survive. Their homework would consist of more of the same, of seeing the truth in life and coping with it

Under the subject. "TRUTH" they learned that first impressions may not be correct.

"Once upon a time," Rachel read, "there was a young rock-watcher. Everyone thought he was odd. At least, that was their very first impression.

They would point at him and whisper, 'That is the boy who watches rocks. By watching a rock, the one jutting out of the water at a nearby lake, the boy learned how to predict the weather very accurately."

'Tomorrow, the sun will be shining," he would say and it came true, just as true as syrup on pancakes. The boats which sailed on the water were guided by the boy's weather forecasting with unfailing accuracy.

When he looked at the rock, many who saw him said. "He is a lazy rock watcher." At least that was their first impression of him.

The boy's eyes were sharp, sharp enough to notice something about the rock. It was growing bumps. Some days it had one bump, two bumps and even five bumps on it.

When he told others about the changing bumps on the rock they became more convinced that he was an odd boy. But the bumps that he saw were the small turtles who came to the rock to rest and enjoy the sunshine. Each tiny turtle looked like a bump on the rock.

The boy liked to think about nature and how it worked. Soon he discovered that the more bumps the rock had the better the weather would become. With no bumps the weather would be windy, cold, cloudy and damp.

If there were five bumps on the rock, the ideal number, then the weather would be about as perfect a day as described by Romantic poets in love.

The boy used a simple logic. More turtles enjoyed being on the rock during beautiful weather. That was how the boy could tell the weather...he counted the bumps.

The turtles came to the rock because they listened to nature; then the boy listened to the turtles."

The children agreed that it was better to use their time listening to nature and much better to think twice about first impressions.

THE ZEPHYR, AN ABSOLUTE ZERO

Len pushed in his nose and simultaneously stretched his eyelids to appear grotesque-looking. He was expressing privately his own personal feelings toward the motionless figure which he felt obligated to watch through a large convex mirror.

"What an absolute zero ," he exclaimed. Len was looking at a dollar bill on the floor next to the Zephyr's bed. Doc dropped it there three weeks ago, on purpose.

"He seen it every day but he never touched it."

"Guess his values are his own, Len."

"He needs aerobics badly, Hal. Think Doc would hate us if we dusted his laundry with itching powder?"

Len, who needed the convenience of two chairs, was in comfortable form as he placed his two thumbs in his ears and began to wave at the mirror.

"Hal, c'mere, quick."

Hal was looking.

"He stuck out his tongue at me."

"Didn't see it Len."

"No really, he stuck out his tongue, just as I gave him the rabbit cars. Maybe he saw you..."

"Naw...he sees a shiny mirror; he sees himself. It's a coincidence. Len, forget about it."

"You think he tongued himself?"

"Yeah, yeah, he tongued himself, Len...Oh, oh somebody is coming.."

Hal heard rapid footsteps climbing the 40 marble steps.

"Bzzzzzzt"

Hal pressed two red buttons, then checked his watch.

The Jogger was back on time.

Doc prescribed 5 miles of running each morning, 5 at noon and an extra 5 miles every evening for Tristan.

TRISTAN IN ORKWAY

At the Knoe airport, Tristan dismantled a special moment with three words. The crowd believed they deserved a "thank you," at least for offering that ennobling, tumultuous moment to the runner. Instead, they heard a shocking. "I DESERVE THIS."

The crowd was not prepared to give an ideal moment. They wished repayment. They preferred recognition. They wished to be bribed with a "thank you," The tenet reigned supreme, "You don't get something for nothing."

The Group Mind prevailed. Now it was resorting to the law.

"I gave two moments, moments for peace," Tristan pleaded. What in him conjured up the moment, or why he implemented it could not be fathomed by his prosecutors.

The judge grappled with the same influence which shattered the moment at the airport. He called it "the motive." Because a motive had to exist, bribery and conspiracy must have occurred. He could not grasp the moment where something is done with no strings attached, not for money, but for a nobler purpose, for God and peace.

A puff of white smoke came through the chimney signaling the decision of the court.

Tristan was pleased at what the Judge ordered: two trim, athletic Policemen assigned to escort him to Orkway. The trio were seen running across Knoe Square, up Willow, and out into the suburbs.

Some said the judge was considerate, others said he was kind but to Tristan, because he was feeling special, it was his moment. For that moment, he was a winner.

Tristan continued his running, up and down the corridor in Orkway.

The gouging, writing, smudging of hearts, ink spills, arrows and initials on the wall above the Zephyr's reclining form gave testimony of its numberless occupants. Len reached for a pencil.

"Can I give him this?" he asked Hal. "Maybe he'll do some art work."

"..Or stab himself."

The slender object fell to the floor.

"Rumors are flying about the place shutting down. Be tough on us little guys."

"I'm already moonlighting at the truck stop."

"I'll probably go into meals full time."

The back and forth jogging of Tristan ceased. He decided to run in one spot, precisely in front of the suicide cell.

Hal and Len watched closely as the Zephyr stirred.

"Thup. thup. thup; thup, thup. thup." the joggers shoes bounded against the floor.

"Thup, thup, thup," the sound continued.

One eye of the slumbering man opened. Then the other. Then he shut both eyes again and turned his back on the scene.

"Thup.lhup.thup," appeared to be everlasting.

Tristan smiled as he saw the Zephyr stand, groggy. He took a step, two, then three.

Then one leg went up; then another..up and down; up and down.

The Zephyr was jogging. But he was not standing straight, he was slanted.

At last Zeph Plover was handed his property. Doc Proud make the decision to return two razor blades to the King of Suicide Attempts as he continued to jog daily with Tristan. Tristan was Orkway's champ in classic endurance running but the Zephyr was first in slant-body running.

At last, the leaden body in the suicide cell, the un-numbered, became activated, even challenging the great Tristan Roe who had run in the prestigious Helsinki races. Down the cell corridor both would dash, one straight; one slanted, day after day.

Tristan, with faith in the wonder of the given moment and his God-given talent, was happy that he could give another the opportunity to be a somebody. Tristan knew he was dispensing an important medicine to his running partner, a good feeling. Whoever had a good feeling about himself is likely to enjoy it and may wish to sustain it. If he enjoys at least some part of himself, he will not kill himself, Tristan reasoned.

Doc Proud had faith in the same reasoning when he returned the cutting implements to the Zephyr.

Tristan was, if not the creator, the practitioner of the "moment." The Knoe students found it fascinating because it came closest to peacefulness.

When Rachel Brink's class was notified of the whereabouts of Tristan, they immediately executed the Fallen Sparrow Operation.

The students keyed their visit to Value and Importance with a special "thank you" to Tristan for popularizing the "Moment."

They lined up neatly, five to a row in front of Tristan's cell while he paced.

"Thank you for the moment," they sang.

"It is a kindness act
With care and warmth imbued:
It brings together, you and I
And generates a loving mood."

With a profound faith in the "Moment," Tristan actually stopped moving for an instant to hear the most delightful prognostication:

"Such moments made, if multiplied
Can generate a MOMENT TIDE
And give mankind the urge to say
"PEACE ON EARTH, IT'S MOMENT DAY."

Tristan was touched. To honor a person's devotion to a belief he holds dear was about the most generous compliment anyone could receive...and from his own kind, students who could be his brothers or sisters.

The students clapped as Tristan made a perfect somersault in tight quarters.

Except for an exchange of autographs the class turned around, facing the Zephyr.

It was an awkward encounter, the students feeling that they should say something.

"Hello." was the extent of their social dexterity.

"Let's sing Second best," suggested Miss Brink, thinking of giving a moment of importance to the prisoner.

The group lined up neatly, lifted their chins and awaited Miss Brink's go-ahead nod.

The Zeph stood, stopping the performers in their track, as he looked into their eyeballs.

"1 am the best," he said resolutely, spitting the last word like a cobra shooting venom. The horde of little mouths dropped as the Zephyr demonstrated his slant run.

MEMORIAL DAY

It's Memorial Day, twelve noon.

Just as the cove meets the river's edge, a crowd gathered to celebrate the inception of Bullfinchtown.

Some with binoculars, some merely shading their eyes to get a better look, they peered upon a vast liquid field, The Mighty Missouri. Their eyes were focusing on two boats far out.

It was the custom of the townsfolk to gather once a year and see a replay of the gun duel between Smith and R.R.Bullfinch. Since that historical event occurred on ice, it was. of course, impossible to recreate during May.

Two boats were chosen as stand-ins. Instead of men, the boats would do the feuding, firing miniature canons at each other.

People checked their timepieces. Then they checked the boats. Nothing was happening.

Seth Culp, the main speaker, had been the object of parental disenchantment recently. On this Day of Remembrance his popularity was about to suffer additional tarnishing as seconds turned into minutes and the boats began floating like pieces of driftwood, downstream.

Those who heard the Mayor say, "The powder was never wet before." did not respond with benevolent understanding. Their one track mind was on a "boom." a puff of smoke and a sinking ship. They were cheated.

"Hi John."

"Hi."

"Hi Jake."

"Hi."

The Mayor wiped his forehead.

"Hi Bill."

"Hi."

"Hi George."

"Hi."

As the crowd began its plaintive mile trek across grassland spotted with struggling Russian Olive, toward Knoe Town. Seth Culp appeared dejected.

"Hi Mayor."

Two welcome voices, perfectly synchronized greeting him from the rear.

He metamorphosed instantly into a smiling, cordial human being. "Oh, it's just you," he said with a dearth of enthusiasm as his head turned, looking at Isidore Krasno and Harvey Calsbeke.

"What? No personal, first-name greeting?" Isidore asked

"That's all I've been doing. ..It's been "<u>Hi.Hi.Hi</u>" but nobody called me Mayor. Know what that means?"

"No, what?" asked Isidore.

"It translates into a vote for the opposition."

"You're misinterpreting. Seth... You're tired. Go home... try some of your wife's chicken noodle and take a nap," advised Harvey.

"...and this fiasco. No "boom" or puff of smoke. When people dress up in their finest and expect excitement and it fails, they don't forget."

"Well, we'll call you Mayor any time. Mayor," quipped Isidore.

"..But you don't count, I mean..."

"Aha, taking us for granted." interpreted Harvey, as the three men proceeded slowly northward.

"Queenie thinks I count."

"My girl friend thinks that I count." said Harvey.

"We both have a positive-minded support person and you, Mayor Culp, do you have a positive-minded support person?"

The Mayor walked with his head down.

"Politics is like courtship," Harvey stated. "Offending is taboo. The days of courtship are days of super caution also.

Courtship is not a fair cross-section of life...You don't want to make 'em mad but they should be made mad. How else will you know if they throw things, slap your face, or get depressed and cry?"

"I say 'I love you" a lot which is an accomplishment for me, Isi... no, I couldn't hurt her."

"When Myra and I dated, I'd come to her home. She'd turn on a T. V. program, family type. I'd flick it to cowboys, detectives or mysteries... my preferences. She'd click it back. 1 would gracefully push her hand off the knob, making it crystal clear that eventually, the house would be mine and the TV would be mine because it went with the house. So, when I told her to get her soft Palmolive-scented hands off my TV, she'd say, 'Yes, Discus Honey' in the sexiest, most thrilling voice imaginable."

"Wow." exclaimed Harvey, "what happened next?"

"She flicked the TV back to her own channel as we looked at the drab, homely Family Show.

"Answer me this, Isi. How do you know the time is right?"

"Right for what?"

"To get married,"

"Between me and Myra, one minute we didn't know, the next minute we did. We frequently took walks past the water shed, east of town, through Chokecherry Ridge and on to the New Ulum Pasture. People who saw us called us 'stock car,' cause when we walked, we would bump each other. We did a lot of bumping...it was our courtship style.

Once when Myra was walking behind me, shielding herself from the brisk wind, it happened."

"What happened?

"I farted."

The Mayor chuckled.

"You what?'

"I farted. That's when I knew it was time to marry.

I used to think too much about getting married....just think and think.... Well, if you let it up to a fart to make the move, then you don't have to think. It can lead you down the right path every time, like a horoscope."

THE WIND SPEAKS

Isidore. Harvey and the Mayor trudged across a half mile of browned, rolling field. They stretched out on the side of a hill, just across Witch Creek, beneath a large, wafting willow.

"A truly serene place," sensed the Mayor as his eyes felt heavy and his body relaxed.

Suddenly, he was enlivened by a voice speaking to him, but no one was in sight. Isi and Harvey had gone.

The wind blew briskly through the long, swinging branches.

"There it is again," reacted the Mayor.

Excitedly he called to the others-

Isidore and Harvey hurried from below the hill where they were cooling their feet in Witch Creek water.

"What is it?" Isidore asked breathlessly.

The Mayor didn't move, not an inch from his original position

"Listen." he said.

The three men listened...but nothing

Isidore sat down and again all three men listened closely.

A gust was playing with the whipping branches.

A minute passed.

"Hear it now?"

"Yeah... sounds like "loves you.'"

Harvey was amazed.

As the wind began blowing from every direction the message became clearer.

"I've got it now," shouted the Mayor. "God loves You." The tree is saying "God loves you."

Until dusk, all three grown men relaxed, listening to the wind. They were separated from the rat race as effectively as if they were never born.

CINDY IS NO MOOSE

"Moose" is the name of a large animal found in heavily wooded areas in the Northwest.

"Moose." was also the name of a pretty girl, a graduate of Miss Brink's class. She had a slight separation between her front teeth, just like her father. She was no different from an ordinary kid and resembled a Moose only because she had big feet. She didn't feel that justified the name, and protested it in Family Government The moon would sooner split in two than to have a bunch of brothers rescind that ugly name. The vote was always 5 to 1, against rescinding.

Cindy "Moose" Suzanne Proud was exceptional for a kid her age. She had a conscience. She wouldn't lie. She never cheated. She was only 15 and her word was a good as gold. She liked the ways of Tristan, especially giving moments.

Cindy was instinctively drawn to people who had more than their share of losing. Last Summer she had spent her vacation in Jamaica helping the poor children.

Cindy wanted the meek to prevail. She went to the downtown missions carrying a box, singing:

"If you lost all you own.

Come and get your ice cream cone."

It was all she could afford, finding pop cans strewn about town.

Giving "a moment" by treating someone very special was needed. It was most often welcomed and responded to with a "thank you," but not always. The M.Y.O.B. (Mind your own Business) responses, in particular, were painful and disheartening.

But Cindy didn't give up. She realized that people were victims of that heartless group mind which told them to be on guard against tricksters, that you never get something for nothing, that the bill will come later.

Cindy was in favor of a change in government. Men have had too much power in her life and it was time for her to speak up against this form of favoritism. She could not change the lopsided vote in Family Government but she could help elect a Mayor of the fair sex.

When Ariffa Victoria Plover, with absolutely no political savvy, campaigning on the issue of Orkway and little else, decided to run for Mayor of Knoe Town. Seth Culp realized that his popularity would hit rock bottom. Ariffa had one stinging credential which she posted generously about..."I AM A WOMAN," which pleased Cindy, her number one support fan.

Cindy would pray the usual thanksgiving prayer, mostly because her brothers wouldn't.

"Thanks for mom and dad, for this food and bless the scumbags who live here."

"After the meal Dad proud asked, "Any complaints about mom and dad?"

"Yeah, said Chick, you should ground her for a month."

"How come?" Cindy snapped back.

"You called us scumbags."

"You are."

"There, There...see, see.. Do your job Dad. That calls for punishment for Moooose."

"And what's this about silly Ariffa?" Pude asked.

"'That's Ariffa Veronica Plover...get it right. I'm campaigning for her."

"Who do you know?"

"The street people. They listen to me. I ask them to vote for Ariffa."

"That's stupid," Groove challenged. "She wants to close Orkway, and we all know that Dad works on Orkway."

"Yeah. Moose. Dad will lose his job. then the food will go, then the house and soon we will become grimy street people," concluded Chick.

Dad Proud handed the last empty dish to Mother Proud who placed it into soapy water in the sink.

"Dad will get another job; the Proud clan will survive together; I promise," said the father reassuringly. "Furthermore, Cindy may follow her conscience. I wouldn't want it any other way."

Besides, the Mayor of Littlefield...he'll close Orkway, just as soon as he becomes elected Governor."

"I still think Moose should be grounded." Chick, persisted.

"Now, listen carefully, say after me....Cindy."

"Cindy."

"Good."

"Say after me, Pude ...Cindy."

"Moose."

"I guess I have to use authority here, Guys. Reason is not working. The rule is this: You will not call your sister Moose. It is not appropriate and she does not like it. I will repeat the rule one more time: From now on you will call your sister, Cindy."

Dad Proud walked outside, his only daughter followed. Except for an occasional cricket chirping, the night was sill.

"Thanks Dadio."

"Welcome, Darling Two."

Cindy was Darling Two. Mother Proud was Darling One. There were no other darlings in the Proud Clan between earth and the star-studded heavens.

Cindy talked of God. She was barely 16 and talked of God, the Creator of the Universe.

She found one star in the corner of the sky and pointed. In the opposite corner she found another star and pointed.

"Dad, do you think those two places will ever come together?"

"Doubt it, honey."

"I can bring them together."

"Huh."

"Watch me."

Cindy ran her finger straight across the sky.

"There," she said, "I made them come together."

"You draw a line with your linger connecting the two stars."

"Dad, you realize there is no other creature in the world who can connect two dots and make a line. Isn't it wonderful that people should live and make lines, otherwise the dots would be mere dots forever."

"Who said so?"

"Tristan Roe said so...He's neat...and do you know we are dots as well. When I turn in one spot I say to myself, 'I am here;' and when I am in another spot I say to myself, 'I am there.' When I connect those two dots you know what I've got?"

"Cindy Proud?"

"Right, but how did you know?"

"I guessed."

"Well, the real answer is, I am. That's how you get to be aware of yourself. Imagine that, dad, by checking to see if you are in many places, then you know you are around. ..it's an education you don't get from your regular friends. Oh. by the way...Miss Brink wants to thank you for allowing Tristan to speak to our tenth grade honesty class. He's neat."

".....and two people who are meant to come together begin as two points," continued Cindy. "Once they come together...that's love"

Cindy grabbed her Dad's arm...

"You and mother, you came from different parts of the world, thousands of miles apart"

"Yes, we have."

"You were points, then you were connected...you became a Love Line."

"1 never thought of it that way."

"1 can connect the stars with my finger, but who connected you and mother'.'"

Before her dad could speak, Cindy asked, "What would you do if 1 told you 1 wanted to marry a black man?"

"It's your choice.. I trust your judgment, darling II."

"What part of Africa did Tristan's Relatives come from?"

"South Africa, I believe."

"And Dad, what would you do if I said I was pregnant?"

THE TOWER RESCUE

Father appeared like a diplomat being given a police escort at 60 miles an hour. The ambulance was waiting. Everyone was looking up at a tower, held upright by barely visible wires. Halfway to the top the web of crisscross metal had captured a human.

A spotlight shot upwards, penetrating the darkness.

A large, dark, figure broke through the crowd and lunged at the steel structure. His bare hands began pulling his robust body skyward. A frantic command from above, "stay down, don't come any closer or I'll jump," froze him instantly.

"Tell you what," said Father, catching his breath. "If you jump you'll break a leg or two and maybe cripple yourself ...but that is your decision." The swelling crowd below held its breath. "He's telling her to jump," they whispered.

Father sat as comfortably as possible on a narrow piece.of steel, the crowd urging him to come down, fearing he will tell her to jump again.

But Father knew he was communicating importance to the girl by allowing her to think for herself. The crowd sounded like the mother, offering only a big NO with no alternative.

Father looked up, looking closely, he was pleased as he noticed from the posturing that the urgency to jump was diminished.

"Whichever way you go, that is fine with me. It is your decision." The crowd held its breath as the girl descended by five feet.

"Everybody wants to control my life; my mother. I hate her." The voice trembled.

"But I don't hate her."

"A victim of the rampant NO," father judged.

"Are you my friend?" she asked.

"I am your friend," replied Father

The girl came down. It was over....Father had taken her to a fork in the road. He gave her a choice. Instead of a pure, rampant NO (Don't jump) he added a YES. Now it was easier for her to say NO, I won't jump, because she had something to choose from. The girl was not on the tower to jump, she was on the tower begging to make up her own mind.

TRISTAN GOES TO THE FIRE HOUSE ACADEMY

Having heard of the plight of Tristan, Dolly Dirks turned herself in. She gave her moment and paid a price. Five to ten.

Vouched for by Daniel Proud. Ph.D. as both competent and sane and by Dolly Dirks as a "good Samarium." the Judge found Tristan not guilty.

However, the Judge, completely unfamiliar with the "Moment" found Tristan's behavior uncommon and, therefore, peculiar. Therefore, he placed him in the custody of the Manager of the Firehouse Academy to perform acts of public service.

Tristan was overjoyed. He would remember that Judge, looming above him. He would remember a benevolent gleam in his eye, a red. alcoholic nose. Especially would he remember the act of kindness, imbued in warmth, disguised as restitution. He was truly a "moment" man.

MAYOR SETH ENJOYS THE WILLOW

For days the Mayor visited the talking willow. Though the town was a beehive of people, his value and importance came, almost exclusively, from a speaking wind.

Days have come and gone. Boss's Day. Secretary's Day. Mother's day. Father's Day. Earth Day, Memorial Day, but still there was no Moment Day. For everyone to give to another a kindness "for a moment." Thus the walls and fences stood erect, refusing to give free passage to the White Dove.

A Day to honor The Second Best, those who live, those who have lived and those who will live was worthwhile for the Peace Committee to pursue. The Mayor had no doubt about its celebration as another Memorial Day remembrance...but only if he won the election.

A MIND READFR ARRIVES

Meanwhile, a kind of guru, with a holy face, was camping at Martin Cove. It was father Abe's hobby to evaluate Messiah Faces to judge their authenticity. When he received word of this living Messiah, he wanted to look, eventually.

When it was rumored that the stranger could read minds, Father wanted to see him do it eventually.

He asked Isidore to set up a vigil. There was no problem if the man rested in Martin's Grove, but quite different if he moved into town.

THE ZEPH IS GONE

At the Firehouse Academy Father was orienting Tristan, his new student. His intention was to increase the quality of instruction, incorporating particularly The Art of Moment Giving.

To the satisfaction of Ariffa, the Zephyr was gone. He and Tristan received a special permission to run around Orkway twelve times, three times a day. One day. the orthodox runner returned and the slanted runner eloped.

Doc Proud was amazed at the inner workings of politics. With his ear to the grapevine about town and his eye checking out critical mail, he discovered a complete absence of any repercussions. Nobody seemed to mind that Zeph Plover, an extra-ordinary self-destroyer, escaped.

Of course, that message was welcomed by the soon-to-be Governor as well as the female front-runner for Mayor of Knoe Town. It certainly wasn't because of kinship or political sway but Doc Proud also welcomed the elopement. The dollar bill on the floor, the bait for the occupant of the suicide cell, was gone. Apparently Zeph's values were changing.

THE YAK MAN

For seven uneventful days Isidore spied on the strange man in the Grove. As one day followed the other without change. The holy man became less an object of curiosity, a vagabond, a mere bum.

Then it happened. The man moved toward the town, riding a shaggy, odorous yak. Holding his nose, Isidore came close and looked carefully at his face. The man's countenance was a carbon copy of the Messiah seen in portraits. The peace fullness, serenity, the innocence of his face almost brought Isidore to his knees in adoration.

Scrambling and tripping with excitement, he hurried to call Father as the yak's hooves began clanking on the town's hard pavement.

Father arrived in time to see the crowd pursuing the Yak Man through the streets. He looked closely and noticed someone dutifully walking beside him...a woman. As the figure, who obviously depicted a mother, approached the spot where Father stood, he gasped. "It's Mary Duffy." he blurted

She wanted her mind read, of course. Father concluded, but why did she walk proudly, undauntedly by the undisciplined carnival atmosphere which whirled madly about her."

Father examined the rider from head to foot. He visually measured leg and arm dimensions and then compared them with a former recollection.

He scratched his left ear and shook his head as he squinted in the bright sunshine for another look. It was...it was Foxy Harold Duffy. He had returned home. Mother walking; son riding...it was almost sacred.

Foxy had truly graduated from his mother's shed. Through some unknown quirk of nature and circumstance, he found himself in a remote Tibetan village. Following many days of grueling self-discipline and innumerable sessions of mind expansion and thought control, he learned to read minds.

In time, Father knew the Yak Man's destination, the unkempt, unsightly, unadorned back alley.

Plenty volunteered to have their minds read. Those who laughed and giggled deemed it a charade. Somehow, they expected a Hollywood star would yank off a beard or a drape would fall and a hidden camera exposed.

Together, the people talked with alarm. Their minds were read, but precisely, too precisely. As a stranger, he knew too much. That made him formidable,

Word spread and fear spilled across the alleyways. Becoming an accursed symbol of trepidation, the Yak Man left but the imprint of his hoof marks remained.

Because he knew too much, more than even lovers would share, sentries were posted to contain him.

Anxious moments lingered unabated, seeking transformation. Then it came in the form of a wrath against Seth Culp, the Mayor. At first came low murmuring, then boisterous, uncivil language and, finally, "Death to Seth."

Suddenly, the Mayor's election posters begun wearing a beard, resembling the Yak Man. A civil War cannon was placed near the courthouse, it boomed deafeningly near the Mayor's window before being returned to the Knoe Museum. But most humiliating was the white dove, suspended over Knoe Square...it was painted black.

Some wanted to emulate Hacke Cramm at his worst rather than tell a mite more about themselves.

Beholding the Yak Man's countenance, Father believed all was safe. He would not besmirch a single good name even if he camped in the grove forever. But Father knew, it was not the Yak Man they feared but knowing themselves. They were clothed but feared nakedness too much.

WHERE IS PEACE?

Father looked. Where was peace? Not on the football field, and not in Ihe dissatisfaction of minds who were read.

What status existed in Knoe Town? A leaning toward happiness, perhaps.But every house with every family, every organization, club or society sets up bastions, locked doors, demarcations. musk-oxen perimeters to protect happiness. Where can there be a peaceful society in that array of self-serving protectiveness?

Where lay the condition of the town? Somewhere between unhappiness and happiness. Father judged. He was strongly convinced that man cannot be peaceful defending his status quo, protecting his happiness, being for this and against that; supporting this, defying that: agreeing here, rejecting there; liking here, disliking there.

For peace, a triumphing is required, a triumphing over the defense of happiness. Indeed, Father believed the de-triumphing of happiness was the essence of peace.

WHAT WILL RACHEL WEAR?

Rachel Brink received her invitation to participate in the "Being With" experiment.

But what should she wear? She touched each garment hanging in her closet, and paused. She wouldn't be dancing, dining or teaching.

What does a person wear for no purpose? Where are the fashion designers on this one?

Here spontaneous taste said red or orange color was gaudy, but comfortable. She pulled out a dress that had glamour, best worn with her swan broach and sapphire earrings and necklace; and the neckline plunged and plunged. She was ready "to be" seductive.

Then she noticed a super modest item, closed around the neck, hanging clear past the knees. It should eliminate baser associations in men who needed to concentrate on intellectual matters.

Following one hour of decision-making Rachel fell down backwards on the bed, worn out.

She picked up the phone and called a man for help.

Father Abe answered.

He told Rachel wisely, that she was choosing unimportant from unimportant by choosing one dress over another. He suggested, rather, that she choose between important and unimportant. She should choose between sending a dress over with her in it or coming over without wearing a dress.

No sooner did she hang up the phone, she was off blinking her eyes. Then she closed them entirely in front of her clothes closet. She reached out and instantly grasped her exclusive "Being With" dress.

BEING WITH

Some place, under a spired structure which reached heavenwards, was a gathering of six people. Mellow chimes of some unseen timepiece enchanted the adventurers, welcoming them to the provocative challenge of "BEING WITH."

What happens when people come together for no definable purpose? "Where do we start?" "What do we do?" "What do we say?"

They were uneasy. Surely someone would wish to strive to survive, Father thought. He didn't wait long.

Rachel began showing concern for her survival. The label, "A minister's wife." was offensive to her because she was not married to a church. She deplored "housewife" because she was not married to a house. "I think I'm a good teacher, but not a scholar but I can be a better teacher."

"Poor thing, nobody said to "do better"...there she goes, trying to survive."
"You are valuable. The best right now; and you don't have to prove a thing."

"But how can I pay you back for your kindness, Tristan?"

"Poor thing, Tristan mused, "She feels so unworthy. No repayment is necessary. Mrs. Brink, whatever 1 give to you it's yours, you are deserving of it."

Rachel was captivated by the endless provisions of moments for her survival. "It's a nice world we live in," she said thankfully.

Tristan left the room briefly. For some strange reason, his urge to run was absent. He returned with six apples, "Compliments of Father's refrigerator."

"No, countered Father, "Not mine but ours; what's mine is yours."
Harvey. Isidore and Rachel said their "thank you's" in turn.
Father Abe and the Mayor glanced at each other... neither was offering a "thank You."
"I didn't say it because I deserved the apple," explained the Mayor.
Father added his, "me too."
"You deserve it most abundantly," Tristan reassured.

No one was swearing under his breath or had a disgusting looking face or reprimanded, 'conceited,' or even implored: 'be humble, be meek.' No one, for, with this group of six, you could get something for nothing.

"Freedom, I'm feeling free; precious, adorable freedom:" Some relieving experience was taking hold of Rachel.

Father suggested that she was feeling free to know herself without being fearful of the consequences.'

"Yes, that's it," Rachel replied. "Free as a soaring eagle, free to go, free to come, free to be worthy, to have happiness, to be selfish," she went on. "What a beautiful heresy, to be comforted by the freedom of knowing that I am replete with selfishness."

In her effervescence, Rachel thought expansively, as if she had suddenly broken loose form a lifetime of servitude. She wanted to run and voice it somewhere, then settled down proclaiming only: "We're truly selfish sons-of-bitches."

A pall of peacefulness fell over the group....there was silence and a relishing of the silence.

Harvey passed a basket around. Coming to each, an apple core was heard, giving a hollow thud as it struck bottom. No one thanked him; no one had to; everyone deserved it.

The silence was creeping in. Nothing could restrain it; nobody wanted to.

"The more value you place on a person, the less you expect him to give you something in return," Rachel commented leisurely. She called hers, "a penetrating statement, worth the whole journey."

Harvey noticed her "being for" comment and promptly rushed in with a pure "Being with:" "I'm so glad you're here with me." he said. You don't require any reason."

"Well, I must treat you differently because I value you highly," said Rachel, still refraining from having something for nothing.

But no striving was necessary to justify the love she was receiving; no differences were expected.

"Not a single hair on your head would I change," said Father casually. She was succumbing more and more to the protective, love-giving climate of the group, surviving less and less.

The clock chimes were chiming seven times. Six o'clock passed unnoticed. Shoes were shed. Tensions were gone as the room grew heavily laden with silence and unity.

"Is silence an indication that we need not prove anything?" Father asked.

They each appraised the climate:

"I'm very comfortable."

"It's nice here."

"Blossoming here."

"Tranquil here."

"It's a wind, whispering through the pines."
"Its peaceful."
"It's harmonious."
"We don't have to pretend."

The tenacious, clinging silence held fast to the small band, as if it would remain forever.

Eight O'clock chimed. Nobody was noticing.

"We cover up so much with words. We don't need words," observed Rachel. "Is this the climax, the ultimate objective? We have reached a point where we don't have to say anything?"

"That's too easy. I ain't ready for it yet," replied Isidore, feeling an obligation to put more work into it.

"You deserve all the peace of the moment we can give you, Isi," responded Father.

A thick, hard silence descended and lay, unmoving in the room.

Father wondered where those delightful silences went when nobody was summoning them. Perhaps they were always there, permeating the universe, surrounding man, waiting to flow in.

"Where is time?" asked Isidore.
"Gone."
"On the back shelf."
"Who cares."

Is this a sign of harmony with the universe, which is timeless?" asked Father.

"It feels as if time never runs out; it's eternal," Rachel commented . "Harmony is tasting timelessness. but how did we achieve this harmony so quickly?" she asked. "We all feel it; it's as real as anything, it's a secure feeling. Regardless of what pained situation we raise, we have the inviolable assurance that somebody will take care of it."

"We've stopped surviving. Maybe that is why we live." suggested Father Abe, "to reach a point where we stand on a precipice, peer into the universe and see or own non-human existence: peacefulness, timelessness, harmony and silence. It is beyond dog-eat-dog, it is beyond happiness itself; it is experiencing BEING."

Rachel considered it as the ultimate, the timelessness of the peace of heaven. "We have come closest to it," she said, ."to be in harmony with nature, with man, and with the universe."

Isidore called it a "Total fearlessness."

For Father it was "a stilled, small voice. God was not in the thunder; God was not in the lightning, just a stilled, small voice. God was a God of silence, demanding nothing."

For Tristan it was a fusion of individual identities, producing a greater, unified identity. He saw the experience as little hammers, forged into a big hammer, a bigger, protective brother.

Father could not help but to think that death was like that. Perhaps the peacefulness represented man's awareness of his non-human existence, a glimpse into eternal harmony.

"I feel an undergirding, an under-support," claimed Harvey, "which will help me fulfill the purpose of better living in the rat race, yet no one had told me I should be better."

The chimes rang out 12 times. Only father heard what he was hearing. Four times in that chiming he heard: "Earth is peaceful, earth is peaceful, earth is peaceful, earth is peaceful." The long-awaited message seemed to come from somewhere distant. Father was wiping his eyes. Here was his peaceful society, six people together, involved in the timelessness of eternity, the 12th hour being like the first minute and the first minute like the 12th hour.

The last time he cried was at his Father's funeral. Abruptly, he plunged two fat fingers into his coat pocket and removed an old leather comb case. He removed his father's last words from the case, crumpled the paper, and burned it in the palm of his hand. He clapped his hands once and the black pieces of charcoal scattered to the four winds. Then he sat back and looked toward heaven, still bathed in infinite love. God.

At last, Father Abe knew what living was for: living was not only a rush into life's adventures... it was experiencing life and death simultaneously.

Life was coming down to the level of death, not fleeing from it, down from an ever ascending ladder of proofs for survival. When life was not triumphing over death, it received the best that death had to offer, tranquility, harmony, timelessness, security. When life gave up its conditions for survival, death began sharing the infinite love of the universe.

The purpose of life was beyond a conditional happiness merger between people. For Father it was an unconditional peacefulness merger between life and death.

What was peace? Peace was the condition of man not triumphing over man, life not triumphing over death. Except for the triumphing, peace was in every home, in every neighborhood, in every town and city; peacefulness was everywhere on earth and everywhere in the infinite universe.

GIANT'S DESPAIR

It rose up from the plain, the promontory, shaped like a cone. If it stood among many hills it could be called a hill, but isolated on the plain, it was a mountain. A road came straight down, then, like an elbow with the arm bent, it swerved. It was just there, at Devil's Elbow that Father found what rumors had spoken of. Sending Father Abe to check the spot, Doc Proud was not believing it happened, but there it was, right before Father's eyes. It was a white cross festooned with faded red roses, the inscription written on a piece of T-shirt cloth, held up by an oak branch driven into ,the soft clay: PLOVER LIES HERE. IT SAID, THE ZEPH IS DEAD.

To the precipice, one familiar to Father, who traversed it often during his youthful, energetic years at huckleberry-picking time, the Zephyr drove his hearse. There he waited. Those who saw him said, "For two days"...and then he turned that death-carrying machine. For one more day it pointed downward, angled steeply, almost as if poised to fall from the sky, as if held back merely by a piece of cheap twine. Then, they said, he yanked the brake loose, lay down like a proper corpse, and felt the inevitable power of speed intensify.

THE HUMAN FAIR

The most brilliant scholars within the walls of Knoe College gave fresh life to the first volume of "How to be With Someone," as they formally introduced it as a requirement in Advanced Honesty.

The yearning for a dab of peace seemed innately desired. Most in the town of Knoe dropped chores and implements of work as they sauntered over lo Father Abe's Garden of Being whose entrance portrayed a huge sign, suspended by two hefty poles on either side, reading, THE HUMAN FAIR. There his force of Firehouse-Academy students, prepared in the art of Being With, would pair off.

Initially some townsfolk, having experienced the Yak Man's power, feared exposure of their naughty side. They, who held back, inquired of others, "What do they do?"

"It was a pairing-off experience," they were told. "You pair off with a stranger over at Rover Creek and you stay with him in the Garden of Being....and you don't talk." The no-talking was hard," it was against the grain of social expectation.

Within that domain, basked in the warmth of moments of contentedness, resistance melted and the ordeal was perceived as "kind of nice for a change."

He who slouched, bent over, peering with one eye; he who was unable to work due to a phobic fear of lifting; he who sat and watched the growth of grass through a darkened basement window.....all were chosen by Father because each was adept at saying nothing.

Because of the premise, "All is well," no elaboration was required Asking a question would be futile because no response was forthcoming and explanations for wrongdoing were irrelevant because all was forgiven. All were nice; all were good enough.

"Being With" someone unconditionally, no strings attached, no repayinent..that was at the heart of the Human Fair.

Daily the citizens of Knoe stood along side others at work, in businesses, at home, but rarely did they know the feeling of "Being With." Now, some of the most super-charged go-getters, relentlessly driven by power and riches were going nowhere, soothed by a sublime standstill and, ironically, getting TO THE APEX OF

HAPPINESS faster. They experienced even beyond happiness...and, amazingly, it was free. Soon they would be caught up in the whirlpool of relentless consumerism and wild-eyed competition and again live the life of pawns being blown by the chilling breezes of "Being for " and "Being against". The rat race would envelop them until they stepped apart and again felt the blissful contentment of the Human Fair where their selfishness would become completely disarmed...In that place they would find infinite love and, ironically, infinite selfishness. They would know peace.

Like groping ants, ferreting through an anthill, Father's Firehouse Academy recruits crisscrossed about the country, pitching tents on the perimeters of dog-eat-dog cities, providing samples of the omnipresent p

eacefulness of eternity through the unburdening tool of "Being With."

THE LEFT JERKER

But the Human Fair had a second prong. The parking meter, a contrivance to increase income was recruited to provide a caring. Until then, it had one purpose, to receive a coin followed by a right jerk. To its nature was added a left jerk, which had but one meaning, a call for human contact. A red, flashing bulb, would alert a Left Jerker. They were called at the Firehouse Academy and, like a fireman rushing off to pacify the rage of a fire, one would dash to the appropriately numbered meter and offer assistance for the troubled mind. It was in this context that Tristan Roc was trained. In that education he learned the skill of liking with a flair for uplifting and treating with special care, the skill of entering the caldron of brewing, conflicting emotions and knowing the feel of it, the skill of soothing the worry spots with the salve of reassurance, the skill of bringing his strengths as a lifting device, that not one, but both may rise to a greater positive awareness of self, the skill that he should be less, second best, that another may feel the exotic air, the freedom of the soaring eagle, the very best.

Father Abe had accelerated his dual Human Fair treatment for Knoe Town because a need arose. Orkway was shut down.

MAKING ORKWAY PRETTY

That bleak, rocky bastion stood silently, an eye sore on the edge of town. Then a call came to the Proud residence from Mayor Ariffa Plover. She wanted Daniel Proud to return to Orkway to work. "To make it pretty," she stated. Ariffa wanted Doc to paint the building, not the inside but the outside; not with a single color but yellow, green and purple, her Grandma's favorite colors. She wanted Orkway to look like a checker board.

It was not his preferred kind of work, he told Ariffa. She hesitated. "Pay you the wages of a trained Psychologist with twenty-two years of experience." Doc knew she could do it; she had the connections. But why him? After all, she could get a pro to do it for much less.

Winking at his wife who appeared equally as puzzled as she listened on another line and, for the sake of his family and their needs Doc Proud decided to don the attire of a painter and go to work for pay. He would embellish its tired, drab stones and make Orkway pretty for the Mayor.

On hanging up the phone, Doc Proud began scratching his bald head while momentarily staring at the auburn tiles on his kitchen floor. The Zephyr was dead.? Father Abe saw the cross at Devil's Elbow. But why didn't Ariffa mention it?" he asked
himself.

But he did the same. No "My condolences." or "sorry for your loss:" Why didn't he speak the words. Perhaps he had doubts, questioning the style, the ride, the method of deceasing. The thin, sharp blade had always been the self-destruct tool of choice. And Father said there was no wreckage; what happened to that 28 foot hearse, a wheel here, a piece of glass there.

PLEASANT MEMORIES

Ahh, the sun was setting and two figures sat watching the largest building in the middle of Knoe Town, the Miner's National Bank. The man recalled the sign on top, a red sign with the letters, blinking one after the other. As a child, he sat on that very spot with his Dad and several other men. A men's club of sorts with one small kid. Isidore spelled The Miner's National Bank a thousand times. Sometimes the "N" would bum out; sometimes the "M" during those moments of sitting with big people. Whatever lit up he was there to see it.

Now it was dead completely, time had intervened: the bank became a restaurant: a hotel, a movie theater. Finally, it became a large storage container filled with used furniture.

As Myra and Isidore sat by one another on the cool evening grass, holding hands, kissing intermittently, laughing from a joke or from a tickle, they saw two figures passing through, a girl and boy, bumping into cach other, just walking and bumping. The technique was familiar. It was indeed the Isidore and Myra courting ritual which Isidore shared with numerous members of the male sex including the classic runner, Tristan Roe.

He could tell they were at the getting-to-know-you-better stage and not at the serious should l-pop-the-question stage. There was a distinct difference between side bumps, which had a more superficial, friendship meaning and the serious, we-are-engaged back and front bumps where you run the risk of dislodging a fart.

ORKWAY, THE CHECKERBOARD BOX

With numerous squares painted yellow, green or purple. Orkway was looking like a giant plaything, a checkered box. It was a bit too big to put into a Christmas stocking, though the small children insisted on having one. It should be pretty all the time, day and night. Mayor Ariffa Plover proclaimed. Not less than ten spot lights were positioned around it bathing the colored structure from evening to dawn. In front, colored lights were festooned from one corner to the other and the sign ALL YE WHO ENTER HERE ARE DOOMED FOREVER was retrieved and placed conspicuously above the entrance.

The large oak that stood in front of Orkway was cut down, leaving only a stump 3 feet above the ground.

If Doc Proud didn't know better, he would think that Orkway was getting ready for an opening. But nothing was happening. For a few weeks Orkway stood with its painted squares in view during the day and with flood lights caressing it through the night, giving a sweet-toothed child the yearning to reach in from the top with a huge hand and shovel out a bushel of candies.

In the night the bats fly and the kiwi emerges, the owl hoots and the frogs, if they have a reason to, croak. Crickets and all animals of the night resonated with their specialized tunes as Orkway went dark suddenly. Night visitors came with goggles of special manufacture who set up a moving platform. Some slight chugging noise could be heard as boxes from trucks were placed and thereby lifted to the area of the Day Hall.

The foggy mist rolled over bush and berry and cleaned out every vestige of the figures who labored at the entrance of Orkway until dawn. The smell of nature's ordinary morn carried traces of burnt gas mixed in with a humid coolness. The persevering sun pounded its rays of light and warmth against the fog until it receded into some hole completely, remaining there until another sunset and the ensuing darkness lifted it out.

The force of the previous night returned, a half dozen trucks, with lights out,. Moved slowly to the entrance of Orkway, then stopped. The moving platform in place, larger boxes moved upward, higher and higher, toward the Day Hall. No one spoke; efficiency spoke eloquently. Through the barred windows a slight trace of light had shown revealing ceiling shadows enough to verify that movements were rapid and multiple.

Briefly, a speck of light penetrated the darkness at midnight, striking a box being loaded. "Cutlery, dishes and cooking accessories," Doc Proud read, quickly dropping his pen light into his jacket pocket as he walked off briskly.

As he strode along the narrow walkway leading to a bus stop, Doc wondered: Who had a hand in this? Mayor Ariffa Plover was in Schenectady attending water purification conferences and he knew the Governor was in Angora assessing sheep imports. Perhaps Orkway was simply turning into an oblong, checkered storage bin. But why the stealth, the secrecy? At first it was the yellow, green and purple squares which made it "pretty" then the lights to show its prettiness at night, but now. nobody was caring about "pretty." The aesthetic flair lost its sheen. Doc Proud shared these matters with his wife, conjecturing together until 3 in the morning, both falling asleep still clothed with foreheads touching.

In time, a month later, it was finished. But what was finished? All Doc Proud could be sure of was the escalator. You got a free ride to the lop. No doubt, it was a welcome contrivance for those going to the top, but what was the worth of coming face to face with a large steel door.

Doc Proud shared his concerns with Father at Vivian's over a cup of coffee. They had previously talked about the tragedy at the Giant's Despair and the Zephyr dying there. It was Father who thought it strange that Tristan Roe was unperturbed about hearing the news.

"And Ariffa didn't even mention it when she asked me lo paint Orkway." responded Doc.

"Tristan was always a good Friend of Zeph's, ever since he gave him an 'all-for-you-and-nothing-for-me' moment and gave him a purpose to be alive."

"They practiced running together."

"They competed in the Oslo races, Tristan in the classical run and The Zeph in the slant run. Both won prizes."

"Prizes?"

"Money."

"By the way. Daniel," Crystal has been seen with Tristan "

"I know... hope she uses good judgment., she's only 17.

"Isidore and Myra saw them doing some bumping .."

Doc Proud was relieved to know it was only side-bumping.

THE ZEPH RETURNS

Both men heard a ringing. It was emanating from Doc's inner pocket. He reached for his cell phone, flipped the top back and pressed a button.

It was Harvey Calsbeke, driving down Main. He had just seen a curious vehicle, an old model hearse with brown blotches of rust disfiguring the door in the rear.

"The plate. What's the license plate?" blurted Doc.

Harve couldn't tell. It was dirty.

Coming closer he could see the first two letters vaguely...

"Looks like ZE…"

"The Zephyr. It's the Zephyr...He's alive." he said excitedly.

He wanted Harvey to follow the hearse

"Where are you now?" he asked him

"Tenth and Chestnut."

"Now, where is he now," Doc asked moments later.

"Turning on Willow."

"Now where?"

"Steady on Willow."

Orkway was on Willow. It looked like the Zeph was heading toward Orkway, Five minutes later Doc heard the news: The Zeph's Hearse was on top of a stump.

Doc and Father hurried over.

"There it is," said Harve, who waited for them.

It was the death car of the Zephyr all right, on exhibit, perfectly balanced on its driveshaft.

Father stroked his chin and quietly, pensively looked at one word, drawn on the windshield of the vehicle in bold, yellow letters, REBORN.

RESTAURANTE LE ZEPHYR

A silk purse from a sow's car described the transformation in Orkway. The Zeph had $80,000 inheritance. He combined that with his slant running winnings and there it was, Orkway, Restaurante De Zephyr.

He was reborn, but to be reborn he needed to die. He died symbolically at the Devil's Elbow. He extirpated that part of himself that was self-destructive by letting it die; now he was being reborn.

With the stairs that moved a body upward, it was opening time, a place to dine in the Orkway manner. A couple dressed in most elegant dress, with tuxedo and long gown, were escorted to a cell. Locking the door and being fed through the opening at the bottom was a special treat which naturally included additional cost. To request a light for a cigarette one needed but to yell, "fire in the hole." Eating with handcuffs was also additional. A replica of Hacke's Bell was provided to get the attention of a server. As an appetizer everyone was served Kelp from the South Seas, dried and shaped into a cigar. A cigar sandwich was served with a rhubarb stick shaped like a saw. A five dollar nail was provided to the amorous couple who wanted to scratch a heart or initials on the wall.

Groove, the oldest, started technical school. Soon all the kids would be leaving the nest for a college venture. Facing such prospects for five others was not a happy thought especially if the breadwinner is winning no bread. But Doc and wife Cora had an alternative, a secondary plan, one that existed even as they were choosing each other for mating privileges. Each had a profession. Doc was a Psychologist and Cora a nurse. They were two, so if one didn't have work, the other was available to go to work.

Currently, Psychologists had lost their luster and were being tossed into a cheap basket while nurses were prized and dubbed "The Best." Daniel Proud knew that scenario. It could become reversed later on but, in life, you muster your assets, whatever form they may lake, that you and your family may survive.

The Good Samaritan Hospital was convenient, just five minutes by bus for Registered Nurse, Cora. Wherever there was a perk, the Proud clan would work its way to using it such as one free meal at the hospital and the opportunity to sit and dine with Mom.

Restaurant eating was out; penny-pinching was in.

Doc reached into his mail box. He found an envelope which was entirely yellow, yellow gold. It had no stamp. That meant someone hand -carried it to the mail box. The large letter "Z" printed with care in the center, was clue enough.

Puzzled. Doc sat down on the grass near his Alberta Spruce. This seemed like an act of kindness, of reconciliation, of respect even...But no. he couldn't think that, not from the razor-blade wielding Sociopath.

Holding his breath, Doc opened the envelope carefully and unfolded a letter inside. It was an invitation. He and Cora were invited to the Grand opening of Restaurante De Zephyr, Saturday evening, 6:30 p.m. "Formal attire requested."

The next day, just as Cora returned from work, two professional, efficient-looking persons, both heads held high, as if looking over a tall fence, carrying four suitcases, came to the door. The HH member asked if Dr. Proud was in; the SHH member requested to speak with Cora Proud. They represented the Tuxedo and Gown Depot of Knoe Town and were directed to do a fitting.

Although Daniel and Cora Proud requested details about the benefactor, none were forthcoming. The extent of the HE and SHE couples' knowledge was, "We were told to come."

The surprise was astounding because neither Daniel or Cora were planning to go to the opening evening of Restaurante Le Zephyr. Most sincerely, they were practically dying to go, but could not afford the expense, particularly the formal garb. Daniel turned to Cora and carefully whispered, "This is perfect."

One suitcase was set on the floor, opened, then another and two more. A tape was measuring up and down, around the curvature of Cora's body, since she was the first. A book with gown designs and color choices was reviewed by Cora

She pointed, "This one."

The woman quickly wrote down something on the same sheet where Cora's dimensions were written. As if to remind herself and Cora as well, she read her ownwriting, "Evening gown from Chadwicks; Jessica McClintock Red with white opera
gloves."

Cora nodded affirmatively.

Doc Proud chose a Formal Knight Tuxedo with Nocturnal Naughahide by Squeegee; bow tie. white coal and black pants.

The final fitting would be tomorrow at the Proud residence.

As the fancy clothing people were leaving, the SHE person stopped. "By the way. Crystal's K. Yugvestdotter Couter Gown in blue satin is ready."... "and by the way," the HE man said, "a limo will arrive promptly at six on Saturday"... and the SHE person said, "a dozen orchids will arrive at five. "Furthermore," both He and SHE spoke together, "the tuxedo and gowns are yours to keep and. Furthermore, .. the limo is yours."

Doc Proud, Cora and Crystal Proud left the Stretch Limo, all looking elegant and refined. The doom sign was there and, above it, in blinking lights the new name of Orkway, RESTAURANTE LE ZEPHYR. They walked past a hearse, delicately balanced on top of a stump and. waiting at the entrance, was Tristan Roe. Crystal's escort.

The four stepped inside and were instantly transported upward. The huge gate amomatically unhinged itself, allowing the foursome to immediately enter into the Day Hall. Many people had already arrived including the Ditties who occupied many circular tables which were draped by a black cloth.

Before the group could be seated, a burst of applause caught them by surprise. Ariffa was there along with the Governor and they, too, rose to give recognition.

Doc Proud could neither explain the incredible generosity of someone nor these behaviors; nor would he understand why some wanted his autograph.

Political figures with their female partners waved from cells and offered greetings as the foursome was shown to a table at the farthest end of the corridor.

Somehow it didn't seem ominous without that huge 5 ton door and Doc didn't mind entering cell 20. This was a different world. In the middle of the 9 by 9 was a round table, borrowed from a Round table Club of Belgium and the cement floor had been replaced with solid oak. A Tamarind curtain of semi-sheer voile fabric closed behind them as they sat comfortably and snuggly in their private cubical. There were no bars on the one window which had a drape of light, garlic-peach which draped to the floor. A light with a round fixture hung down from the tall ceiling suspending itself exactly above the middle of the table.

After an assessment of the environs, Doc looked nowhere except at his wife and stroked his head in disbelief. Then he asked Cora for a pinch, to wake him up.

Tristan looked nowhere except at Crystal. A bottle of cognac within reach of everyone remained untouched as Cora played with an empty glass.

Events were transpiring too rapidly for Doc to comprehend fully. Why would people he hardly knew, those who were dining in Orkway's cells, be congratulating him...and what for? ...And why the "Good Lucks?" Did they know he had no job and had recently gone to the Court House for a handout of government cheese?

The curtain drew back and there, standing in a black vest and white shirt and bow tie, was none other than the Zeph. He gave each a menu, being accompanied by two assistants, similarly dressed. No familiarity was expressed. It was a quiet, professional interlude. "I will be your server," the Zeph said politely, holding a white cloth over his forearm. "May I recommend Baku flying fish and Armagnac spider crab with Matzo bread? For dessert, Babau Rhum Sponge cake soaked in rum syrup. ..He shook his head in wonderment and delight, opened up the menu, and just that quickly decided on some Jerusalem Artichoke, cheese from Savoi and prime rib.

The dining was over...then came the chant that runners who were present could not resist..."RUN, RUN, RUN."

Tristan rose from the table.

"Be careful, you just ate," Cora said with motherly concern. The corridor was cleared. There they stood, like two penguins in waiter's outfits. A"GO" sounded, and they were off. One classical and one slant runner gave the guests a treat. Twelve times: One dozen times they ran the length of the corridor.

The Zeph won.

Panting lightly, the slanted runner returned to cell 20. "I have received value and worth," he said, speaking to Dr. Proud. I was a nobody. Then I received a "moment" and it was free. That moment meant everything to me. Tristan tapped my talent...a talent to call my very own. That special caring of another just for me was a kindness which, at first, 1 did not see.. On top of Giant's Despair, nearer to heaven, I sat. At the bottom I died to selfishness; on the top I was reborn to the "Moment." So, Doc Proud, because I'm satisfied with just enough, I give you my moment, my life's earnings, my everything for you and nothing for me: Congratulations, you are the new owner of Restaurante Le Zephyr."

Doc Proud looked at his wife in disbelief. There was no logic because he deserved none of it.

Then the Zeph reached into his pocket and handed Doc Proud two double-edged razor blades. From inside of his coat he lifted a Bible and said, "1 have found someone to emulate, a God who gave me His Moment, His all, just for me."

HAIL HAIL.HAIL TO THE SECOND BEST, resounded down the hallway as the Ditties grouped together in song.

What I give I give free
For now and for eternity
East and North and South and West
I've been good, but you are best...
Hail Hail Hail to God's Second Best
Who make the Best prevail.

------Finis-----

Contact: job_elizes@yahoo.com - tatay@usa.com - Publisher's Other Books:

Writings 1 Book, 2009 + + I. Catch That Story, *Tatay Jobo Elizes* + + II. Obit, *Bambi Harper* + + III. Speech, UP, 2003, *Butch Jimenez* + + IV. Speech, Silliman U, 2006, *Butch Jimenez* + + V. The Mission Moment, *Dr. Phil Stack* + + VI. Writing Underground, *Mila D. Aguilar* + + VII. Academic Freedom, *Mila Aguilar* + VIII. Subanon Spirits of Rice & Land - *Noel Cornel Alegre* + + IX. I Look Out The Window - *Atty. Toto Causing* + + X. Ride On A Bus, Poem, *Melanie Ferrer & Friend* + + XI. Why Am I Doing This, *Susie Barbieri* + XII. How To Court A Philippine Lady, *Rodel Ramos & Jose Torres* + + XIII. Inspiring Young Filipino Entrepreneur, *Lloyd Luna* + + XIV. The Success Story of Ian Del Carmen, *Lloyd Luna* + + XV. Story of Bacna Surgical Mission, *Sylvia Salvador* + + XVI. 1987 Philippine Constitution, *Full Text (Special Feature)* + + XVII. Why Publish Writings, *Tatay Jobo Elizes*

Writings 2 Book, 2009 + + I. Why Can't We Act Up Together, *Susie Barbieri* + II. I Know Where They Are All Going, *Cesar Lumba* + III. There Is Hope For The Philippines - *Grace Padaca* + + IV. Pointers On Employment Abroad, *Melanie Aquino* + + V. Without KNCHS: (Love story), *Atty. Toto Causing* + + VI. 422 Years Ago, *Rodel Rodis* + + VII. Filipino American History Month, *Rodel Rodis* + + VIII. Love is the Next Truth, poem, *Daniel Rodil* + + IX. A Need For Reflection, Gloom, *Cesar Torres* + + X. Our Purpose Driven Life, *Joey Concepcion* + + XI. Did Ninoy Die For Nothing, *Joey Concepcion* + + XII. Why The Filipino Voted, *Pablito Lim* + + XIII. Life And Love, Poem, *Nannette Yatco* + + XIV. Criteria - American Institute of Philanthropy, *Charity Guidelines (Feature)* + + XV. Strangers In Our Own Country, *Casiano Mayor Jr.* + + XVI. Coming Revolution In The Ballot, *Cesar Lumba* + + XVII. 2009, A Retrospective, *Cesar Lumba* + + XVIII. All Over The World, *Vicente Rivera Jr.* + + XIX. Harvest, *Loreto Paras Sulit* + + XX. Things Your Burglar Won't Tell, *Jude Tagaciudad* + + XXI. The Gypsy Soul, *Casiano Mayor Jr.* + + XXII. An End To Cheating, *Sonny Coloma* + + XXIII. Toward Culture of Giving, *Sonny Coloma*

Writings 3 Book, 2010 + + I. EPIC25, Emerging Philippines Investors Coalition, *Norman Madrid* + + II. Management Ability As An Issue, *Dr. Rene B. Azurin* + + III. Do We Really Want To Give Our Politicos More Power, *Dr. Rene B. Azurin* + + IV. Will 2010 Fulfill High Hopes For Better Life, *Ernie D. Delfin* + + V. Comelec Is The Root Of All Evils, *Toto Causing* + + VI. Advantages of Federalism/Parliamentary, *Dr. Jose Abueva* + + VII. Sometimes A Great Nation, *Mar-Vic Cagurangan* + + VIII. Great Conspiracy, *Mar-Vic Cagurangan* + + IX. Of Speech & Life's Riddles, *Casiano Mayor* + + X. Bad Start To The Year, *Rod Garcia* + + XI. A Dinner Out, *Rod Garcia* + + XII. One More Time, *Roy Gaane* + + XIII. Musings, *Ceres Busa* + + XIV. Value Formation For Good Citizenship, *Roger Reyes, JMC Nepomuceno, Ramon Gonzales, CDVictory, Mila Marzon* + + XV. On Being Filipino American, *John Reyes* + + XVI. The Monterey Peninsula, *John Reyes* + + XVII. The Salaza Fiesta, *John Reyes* + + XVIII. Salawikain: Filipino Proverbs, *John Reyes* + + XIX. Musikero (The Musician), *John Reyes* + + XX. Strange Noises, *Tatay Jobo Elizes*

Writings 4 Book, 2010 + + I. The State of Our Nation and Democracy In 2010: Building 'The Good Society" We Want, *Dr. Jose V. Abueva* + + II. Assessing Expanded Role of AFP in Nation Building, *Col.Dennis Acop, Ret.* + + III. Assessing RP's Security Strategies Alternative Views, *Col. Dennis Acop, Ret.* + + IV. The Way We Were, *Fred Natividad* + + V. Veterans of Ipo Dam, A Fiction, *Fred Natividad* + + VI. A Plea, *Miguel Reyes Reynaldo* + + VII. Int'l Youth Bowling, My Impressions, *Marjorie Ann Elizes Reyes* + + VIII. Mi Ultimo Adios (My Last Farewell), *Dr. Jose P. Rizal* + + IX. Aling Pagibig Sa Tinubuang Bayan, *Gat. Andres Bonifacio* + + X. Rekonsilasyun Dula (Reunion in Heaven), A Play, *Irineo P. Goce (KaPule2 or Leonidas P. Agbayani)* + + XI. Forgery of Rizal Retraction, *Irineo P. Goce (KaPule2 or Leonidas P. Agbayani)* + + XII. Maikling Kasaysayan Ng Malas Na Bayang Pilipinas, *Ireneo P. Goce (KaPule2 or Leonidas P. Agbayani)*

Writings 5 Book - "Best Hopes" 2010, About President P-Noy + + I. The Challenge of a Hundred Days: Believing that Filipinos can, *Tony Meloto* + + II. The 2006 Ramon Magsaysay Award for Community Service, *for Tony Meloto* + + III. Open Letter to Noynoy, *F. Sionil Jose* + + IV. A History of Pain, *Juan L. Mercado* + + V. An Open Letter to Noynoy, *From OFWS* + + VI. Pursuit of Good Governance Advocacies, *Marcelo Tecson* + + VII. A Fervent Prayer for Peace, *Cesar Torres* + + VIII. A History of Betrayal, *Perry Diaz* + + IX.

Corona's Thorny Crown, *Perry Diaz* + + X. Dawn of a New Era, *Perry Diaz* + + XI. Of Mice, Boys and Men, *Philip S. Chua, MD* + + XII. A Hopeful Tomorrow - A Balikbayan Insight, *Philip S. Chua, MD* + + XIII. Global Filipinos: A Sleeping Giant, *Philip S. Chua, MD* + + XIV. Heart to Heart - Winds of Change, *Philip S. Chua, MD* + + XV. Growing Old is a Privilege, *Philip S. Chua, MD* + + XVI. Our Cruelty to Mother Earth, *Philip S. Chua, MD* + + XVII. Advice to Grads: "Never Choose Your Heroes Lightly", *Ernie Delfin* + + XVIII. Gawad Kalinga, A Progressive Movement, *Ernie Delfin* + + XIX. Why a Man Must Save and Invest, *Ernie Delfin* + + XX. Beautiful San Francisco, Pinoy Heaven, *Ted Laguatan* + + XXI. The next President and PAMUSA, *Frank Wenceslao* + + XXII. Philippne Budget Deficit, *Frank Wenceslao* + + XXIII. Money Laundering: US Tools vs. Corruption, *Frank Wenceslao* + + XXIV. Amid the Fighting, Clan Rules Maguindanao, *Jaileen F. Jimeno* + + XXV. Why I Publish Writings, *Tatay Jobo Elizes*

Writings 6 Book, 2010 + + I. SONA, State Of Nation Address, English, *Pres. Benigno Aquino III* + + II. SONA, State of Nation Address, Pilipino, *Pres. Benigno Aquino III* + + III. First 100 Days Speech, Pilipino, *Pres. Benigno Aquino III* + + IV. Finally, Another Ramon Magsaysay In The Making, *Bert Guiang.* + + V. A Covenant With Our President, *Tony Meloto* + + VI. From A Grateful Heart, A Thank You Letter, *Tony Meloto* + + VII. The Scent of Hope For The Global Filipino, *Tony Meloto* + + VIII. Fleshing Out The Broad Strokes, *Felicito (Tong) C. Payumo* + + IX. In Search Of Leaders (Part1), *Felicito (Tong) C. Payumo* + + X. In Search of Leaders (Part 2), *Felicito (Tong) C. Payumo* + + XI. A Conspiracy of Dunces, *Cesar Lumba* + + XII. Only Science Can Solve Poverty, *Flor Lacanilao* + + XIII. Education Reform Amid Scarcity, *Flor Lacanilao* + + XIV. Highblood: Obituaries/Reasons, *Flor Lacanilao* + + XV. How Money Works, *Edmund Lao* + XVI. State of Economy & Society, 2002, *Juan Dela Cruz (Txtmania)* + + XVII. Global Filipinos, *Juan Dela Cruz (Txtmania)* + + XVIII. Understanding Poverty, *Juan Dla Cruz (Txtmania)* + + XIX. Kuyakuy, *Dr. Ramon Marquez* + + XX. Cambodian Octopus, *Joey Jamito* + + XXI. Inspite Of Herself, I Still Love The Philippines, *Joey Jamito* + + XXII. Love Has Wings, *Percy Campoamor Cruz* + + XXIII. Walk For Kris, *Rod Garcia* + + XXIV. Coldblooded, But Alive, *Rod Garcia* + + XXV. It Takes A Village, *Rod Garcia* + + XXVI. Beauty Contest, *Rod Garcia* + + XXVII. Eight Points In Enlightening The Elites, *Orion Perez Dumdum* + + XXVIII. Case Against "Cellphone Revolution", *Sarah Raymundo*

Writings 7 Book, 2010 - My Vintage Pics (Biographical) Tatay Jobo Elizes

Writings 8 Book, 2010 + + I. The Church and the State: In Search of Common Ground, *Gel Santos Relos* + + II. President Aquino: "Walang Kaibigan, Walang Kamag-anak", *Gel Santos Relos* + + III. What Makes Us "Pinoy", *Gel Santos Relos* + + IV. Minsan May Isang Puta (2007), *Mike Portes* + + V. Build Our Dream, *Jose Ma. Montelibano* + + VI. Hope In Europe, *Tony Meloto* + + VII. Wealth in Canada, *Tony Meloto* + + VIII. Parenthood: A Sacred Covenant, *Philip S. Chua* + + IX. Are We, Humans, Really Civilize? (Or, are we for the birds.), *Philip S. Chua,* + + X. Save Our Nation, *Philip S. Chua* + + XI. A Time To Pause, *Philip S. Chua* + + XII. The Gawad Kalinga Virus, *Philip S. Chua* + + XIII. A Marching Order For P-Noy, *Philip S. Chua* + + XIV. "Bayan Ko" Bonds, *Philip S. Chua* + + XV. P-Noy's First 99 Days, *Philip S. Chua* + + XVI. The Practice of Quackery in the Phils, *Cesar D. Candari* + + XVII. Remember When? A Brief History of Old and Recent Past, *Cesar Candari* + + XVIII. The Philippines Before and What Now?, *Cesar D. Candari* + + XIX. The Traffic Problems are Beyond "Wang-Wang", *Cesar D. Candari* + + XX. Behind The Gold, *Eliseo Serina* + + XXI. May Angal? (Any Complaint?), *Greg B. Macabenta* + + XXII. Pagbalik-Tanaw Sa Kapatirang Masoneriya Sa Pilipina, *Irineo P. Goce* + + XXIII. Mysteries & Riddles Behind RP's Corridors Of Power, *Irineo P. Goce* + + XXIV. Wika - Diwa Ng Lahi, O, Ang Tore ni Babel Sa Pilipinas, *Irineo P. Goce* + + XXV. Can There Be Peace; Is There Hope For Progress?, *Irineo P. Coce* + + XXVI. Drama Queen, *Percival Campoamor Cruz* + + XXVII. Ang Tulay na Kahoy, *Percival Campoamor Cruz* + + XXVIII. Sa Alaala ni Maria Lorena Barros, *Percival Campoamor Cruz* + + XXIX. Text Game or Text Gambling?, *Juan dela Cruz* + + XXX. Of Husbands and Wives, *Juan dela Cruz* + + XXXI. It Must Be Love, *Juan dela Cruz* + + XXXII. Elite Triad Blocking Reform, *Demosthenes B. Donato*

Writings 9 Book, April 2011 + + I. Solidarity in Literature W/out Borders, *Simeon Dumdum Jr* + + II. Macario Sakay Vindicated, *Gemma Cruz Araneta* + + III. The Dilemma of the Last Filipino, *Larry Henares* + + IV. Ping Joaquin, Fil. Jazz Pianist, my Father, *Tony Joaquin* + + V. Bert Del Rosario, Inventor, Sing-Along, *Tony Joaquin* + + VI. Xmas Article 2009, *Allen Gaborro* + + VII. Beaches (short story), *Allen Gaborro* + + VIII. Democracy Versus Discipline, *Allen Gaborro* + + IX. Amend the Const. Make Jury Trial, *Atty. Toto C. Causing* + +

Solo Authored Books: + + +

Book A, **Turning Points - Empty Dreams,** *Job Elizes Sr,1968 (Reissue 2009)* + + +
Book B, **Be Considerate - Behaviour Issues,** *Tatay Jobo Elizes (Jr),* 2009 + + +
Book C, **Piglets Unlimited - Wealth Untapped,** *Tatay Jobo Elizes,* 2009 + + +
Book D, **Out of the Misty Sea We Must,** *Cesar Lumba,* 2010 + + +
Book E, **Fulfilled** – *(By His Parents) Gonzales Reynaldo, Editor,* 2010 + + +

Dook F - **Reflections** *- Bert Guiang,* 2010 + + +
Book G, **Writings 7 - My Vintage Pics,** *Tatay Jobo Elizes,* 2010 + + +
Book H, **May Bagwis Ang Pag-ibig,** *Percival C. Cruz* + + +
Book I, **Letters To Matrimony,** *Irineo Perez Coce, Ka Pule2,* 2011 + + +
Book J, **Songs I Wish You Knew,** *Soledad R. Juan,* 2011 + + +

Book K, **Make My Day,** *Larry Henares Jr.,* 1993, Re-issue 2011 + + +
Book L, **Our Guerrero Family,** *Tatay Jobo Elizes,* 2010 + + +
Book M, **Joketor 1,** *Tatay Jobo Elizes,* 2011 + + +
Book N, **FaveArt 1,** *Tatay Jobo Elizes,* 2011 + + +
Book O, **Beyond idle thoughts,** *MLMunoz, Sept,2011* + + +

 Book P, **Cracks In The Armor,** *Mariano Ngan, Oct 2011* + + +
Book Q, **FaveArt 2,** *Tatay Jobo Elizes,* 2011 + + +
Book R, **Balitang Kutsero,** *Perry Diaz, Jan 2012* + + +
Book S, **FaveArt3,** *Tatay Jobo,* 2011 + + +
Book T, **FaveArt4** *,2012, Tatay Jobo* + + +

Book U, **Stack Family Journals,** *Phil & Fe Stack,* 2012 + + +
Book V, **Emily, An Adoption Journey,** *Romerl Elizes,* 2012 + + +
Book W, **Hermes Alegre Art Gallery,** *TJ & Hermes, 2012* + + +
Book X, **Masaya Din, Malungkot Din,** *Jovelyn Bayubay Revilla, 2012* + + +
Book Y, **Tiis, Sipag At Tiyaga,** *Raquel Delfin Padilla, 2012* + + +

Please buy online or give a gift in hard copy or kindle edition. All authors and titles are easy to search, trace or find online. Thanks. Publisher

Tatay Jobo Elizes

www.ingramcontent.com/pod-product-compliance
Lightning Source LLC
Chambersburg PA
CBHW070139290526
45789CB00002B/545